Panther Tales And Woodland Encounters

Seeing is Believing

By Judith Victoria Hensley

Panther Tales
And Woodland Encounters
Seeing is Believing

Judith Victoria Hensley

ISBN-13:
978-1985788350

ISBN-10:
1985788357

Printed by Create Space, an Amazon.com Company
CreateSpace, Charleston, SC

www.CreateSpace.com/TITLEID

Available from Amazon.com, CreateSpace.com, and
other retail outlets

Cover Design: Judith Victoria Hensley
Cover Image: Creative Commons Public Domain

Dedication

To my people, my kin, and my friends who treasure our heritage and oral histories in Appalachia

Thank You

To all those over the years who came forward to share their stories for this book

To those who read and listen to the sincere stories of others without contempt or disdain

To Byron Crawford, reporter, writer, encourager for this project

To Ed Brown, Daniel Benoit, and Jimmy Blanton who deemed this project worthy of air time on their podcasts, and Jennifer McDaniels who made those connections supporting this project

To those who appreciate a good story and a story teller

To the Appalachian Americans Facebook page and its members who freely to my request and shared encounters for this book

Table of Contents

If you have a story about your own eyewitness encounter of a big cat, or a story you know from a reliable source (such as family stories handed down), that you would like to contribute to an upcoming book, please follow the guideline on pages 297-298

Several Reliable Reports
An Interview with Byron Crawford
By Judith Victoria Hensley

Byron Crawford is from Shelbyville, Kentucky. He was the state columnist for the *Louisville Courier Journal.*

"It was a position that had existed for many years, written by Joe Creason, before I took the job. Alan Trout had also been the Kentucky columnist. Our job was to travel the state from one end to the other writing about anything we found interesting that we thought people would like to read about. I did that for nearly thirty years."

Currently, he writes the back-page column and essays for *Kentucky Living Magazine,* which reaches a readership of about 1.3 million Kentuckians. The magazine is a publication of the Kentucky Association of Electric Co-operatives. His page is "Byron Crawford's Kentucky."

When I asked Byron what initially caught his interest about the big cat stories, he said his work on the big cats basically spanned a time period from the late 1970s through 2004 when he retired from the Courier Journal. The original spark of interest was because of a story that came from a highly respected gentleman who was a farmer and extremely well thought of in his community in Henry County in the area of the state that is up around the Kentucky River. This individual was also a very knowledgeable outdoorsman.

The gentleman was feeding cattle one winter afternoon and saw a big cat in the barn lot very close to him. He described this creature very thoroughly as a mountain lion. He also had a neighbor who also saw this big cat a few days or weeks later. They were sure it was a tawny colored mountain lion.

"Between the reports from the two of them describing the same big cat, it pretty well convinced me that something was going on. I had heard some talk before this about big tracks, but their encounters really fired my imagination. This happened in the mid-1970s. My first written reporting on the subject wasn't until the 1980s."

Mr. Crawford reported on a story about a man named Forest Douthitt, a Henry County farmer who came face to face with an animal he believed to be a mountain lion in a field about three miles from the Kentucky River. Mr. Douthitt saw the big cat from a close distance and was quite sure of what he had seen. The cat went off into the woods and there was no sign of it for a while.

A couple of months later, a neighbour named Frankie Dale spotted a big cat at very close range while he was deer hunting along the

Kentucky River. It leaped up the hill and disappeared into a wooded hillside.

Both men were convinced that what they saw was a mountain lion. Of course, people may have been sceptical at the time, but in the years since then, there have been an abundance of reports similar to the two these gentlemen offered. For sceptics, the common denominator of their doubt is the lack of verifiable film, photographs, or the capture of such a cat.

Officials are leaning more toward the possibility that mountain lions are in Kentucky. At one point, the Kentucky Department of Fish and Wildlife compiled a census of fur bearing animals. It was the first such survey of this nature ever conducted in Kentucky.

For the study, 300 scent posts were set up in scattered locations across the state. The post is anchored in the ground at the centre of a three-foot circle that is clear of vegetation. It is baited with animal scent. The census is then based on the animal tracks which are left inside that circle on the designated night.

Many bobcat tracks were found, but one stood out among the others. Although some bobcats can grow to be quite large, this particular print appeared to be the track of a mountain lion.

It was found by Robert Morton of Hazard, Kentucky who was a district biologist for the Kentucky Wildlife Department. He worked in several counties in south-eastern Kentucky. The track was found on Pine Mountain near the Harlan and Letcher County border southwest of Whitesburg. The track was 3 ½ inches wide and 3 inches long. Morton and his colleagues were familiar with the study of cougar tracks and easily identified this track.

Morton jokingly said, "The only way to be 100% sure of what made this track is to see the animal standing in it, then take about four good photographs of it!" However, Morton did believe that the track he found near Little Shepherd's Trail, not far from Highway 119 in Harlan County, was that of a mountain lion, panther, puma, or catamount. (Big cats are known in different places by all of those names.)

The questions put to biologists about the sightings of these big cats in Kentucky is, "Are these big cats really here? If so, why?"

A subcommittee was formed many years ago called "The Panther Subcommittee." It encouraged the south-eastern states in the USA to establish a central location for panther sightings and records of these reports. It was an effort to track where reports came from, to determine if the panther was making a comeback to the region, and if so, what the distribution of the animals was.

Chester Stephens, of Whitley City, in McCreary County was Kentucky's representative on that subcommittee. He reported a story about two loggers on a logging road who both said a large, long-tailed cat jumped out in front of them and ran up the road about 200 yards before running into the woods.

Stephens agreed with others in the field who speculate that cougars which were illegally harboured as "pets" and may have been released back into the wild when the owners got tired of them or could no longer handle them due to size and feeding habits.

Reports continue to come in from across the state of Kentucky over the past few decades. Cougars are elusive animals that do not in general pose a threat to human beings. If there is a natural increase in the big cat population, it may correlate to the increase in the number of deer in the state. Because of the large number of deer present, it is not unreasonable to think the cougar may expand its range.

Other animals that are making a reappearance in Kentucky are coyote, black bear, and even porcupines. Coon hunters in the northern part of the state have had to pick porcupine quills from their coon hounds. Elk herds that have been released in recent years are doing quite well. This makes one ponder, "Why not the big cats?"

Anyone who has had a sighting and wishes to report a suspected mountain lion to Kentucky Fish and Wildlife can call the department's Information Center during weekday working hours at **1-800-858-1549** or by emailing **info.center@ky.gov**

Several years ago, a man from Calvert City names R.D. Norris was on a search for a black panther. Mr. Crawford photographed him with a set of leopard tracks that were similar to what he was trying to find in Marshall and Livingston Counties in the Land Between the Lakes Area.

Mr. Norris believed the black panther inhabited that region of western Kentucky. He collected stories of sightings from farmers, hunters, trappers, and others in the area who reported seeing the big black cat with its long tail. His search was along the Clarks River in Marshall County and in neighboring Livingston County.

Mr. Norris said that most of the sightings reported to him took place in wooded river bottoms where hardwoods and underbrush lined the river. He believed the accounts he recorded to be reliable. He also personally found large tracks and other signs in the area of his search.

John Castle from Birmingham, Michigan spent years investigating the black panther phenomenon. In his research, he made two trips to western Kentucky to discuss the big cats with R.D. Norris. Mr. Castle collected interviews with people who reported having seen large black cats. Based on the reports he received, he believed that some of the "black panthers" people saw were actually black leopards, even though these cats are not native to the United States. He believed that some of these cats may have been released in the 1960s when they were popularly and illegally kept as exotic pets.

Mr. Castle believed that people may have released the cats into the wild when they got too big or too difficult to manage. Many reports came from areas around military installations. From this correlation, Mr. Castle surmised that military personnel may have brought the animals illegally into this country, then turned them loose when they couldn't control them.

Reports about the big black cats or tawny color mountain lions can be found across the state. There was a report from Hawsville in Hancock County on the Ohio River, as well as from Crittendon County which is on down the river from Hawsville.

Although the mountain lion or cougar has long been believed to be extinct, wildlife management officials have begun to take another look at the possibility of the big cat being found in Kentucky. Federal law prohibits the killing of any endangered species.

Leonard Lee Rue III described the mountain lion in his book *Game Animals - A Field Book of the North American Species* notes that the black panther species is seen in Florida.

One of the most creditable witnesses has been a biologist from the Tennessee Valley authority. He described seeing a large black cat between 3 ½ feet and 4 feet long with a long tail that curved over its back. The late-night sighting took place on a Tennessee road near Land Between the Lakes.

Those who believe the big cats exist remain hopeful that proof will be found to validate the presence of the big cats in Kentucky. They hope for paw prints, hair samples, a skull, skin, captured specimen, or other physical evidence that could be sent to and analysed by a scientific laboratory. There is also hope of photographs from tail cams, or clearly identifiable video to verify the stories.

On the Cumberland River in Burkesville, Kentucky (which is close to the Tennessee border), a Labrador retriever was reported to have been attacked by a mountain lion. "It was one of the incidents I wrote about for the *Courier Journal,*" said Mr. Crawford.

Richard and Patricia Keen reported the incident, which happened in their back yard just before dawn on an autumn morning several years ago. Patricia let their dog, Molly, out the back door and put on a pot of coffee.

A little while later, she looked out the back door to check on Molly. This dog and two others who were penned up were all sitting perfectly still and staring in the same direction. Patricia looked in the direction they were staring, and a large mountain lion was lying about 25 feet in front of their pen.

She opened the glass door and the cougar turned and looked at her. Then it got up and started walking toward their garden. She ran and woke up her husband, Richard, to tell him what she had seen.

When he looked, he saw nothing and questioned whether she was sure about the mountain lion. He thought maybe she had seen a deer, which would have been the same color of the animal she described. Deer often came into their back yard.

A little time passed, and the couple was sitting at the table drinking their morning coffee when Richard saw something moving back and forth at the edge of the security light. At first, he thought it was two or three deer moving around in the edge of the light. He couldn't see the whole bodies of the animals but saw the coloring which was like that of deer. There certainly was no danger from a couple or three deer.

Patricia went out the door to the dog pen, thinking all was safe. A few seconds later, Molly bolted up the hill to confront the intruders. At that point, Patricia and Richard both got a good look at the animal, then heard Molly yelping in pain.

When Molly came back over the knoll, Richard saw a mountain lion was in pursuit with two cubs the size of Molly. Molly was headed to Patricia at the dog pen. When she realized what was going on, Patricia and Molly ran for the back door. Richard ran for his gun, but by the time he got back, Patricia and Molly were safely inside and the big cats were gone.

Richard was sure the cat they had seen was a mountain lion. Patricia guessed that from nose to tail, the big cat was about seven feet long.

Molly had suffered two large puncture wounds to her back just above her hips.

When daylight came, Richard and his son (who was a biology and zoology student at Western Kentucky University) found a large paw print in the garden. They made a cast of the print. A local conservation officer measured the track at 4 ½ inches across.

I've been told that staff from the Department of Fish and Wildlife have found big cat prints on Pine Mountain in Eastern Kentucky and have sighted the animal in one or

more locations. They have also spotted the big
cats more than once in the Land Between the
Lakes are of the state.

Officials continue to say that the reports of
mountain lions or panthers in Kentucky is
highly improbable. "Personally, I don't want to
tell anybody who gives an eye witness account
of having seen one of the big cats that they
didn't see what they think they saw," said Brian
Bullock of the Department of Fish and Wildlife.

There was a man in Bowling Green once
who said he had shot an alligator on the Green
River. Most people would have said he didn't,
but he did. It was five feet long. Who knows
how it got there?

(In the past winter, an alligator was found
frozen to death in a yard in Harlan County. No
one knows where it came from.)

Mr. Crawford says he often got letters from
readers about something he had written. He
commented on a letter he once received from J.
L. Willenbrink of Louisville. After reading about
the incident that happened with the Keen
family, he wrote to say that one of his fishing
buddies, Jack Hinckle, of Big Fork, Montana
watched a mountain lion swimming across a
bay at Kentucky Lake in the late 1940s. He had
followed the animal to shore to be certain his
eyes hadn't deceived him.

In June 2004, Mr. Crawford wrote about the subject again. Reports from Henry, Oldham, and Trimble Counties about sightings of the big cats caught his attention. With unresolved questions from his past research and newspaper columns still lingering, he wondered if all these stories had become part of an urban legend, or if there truly is something out there.

Residents near Lake Jericho in Sulphur, in Henry County and around Sligo, Pendleton near the Little Kentucky River, and from the Trimble and Henry County Lines seem convinced that the big cats are out there.

Doctor Jann Aaron owns a farm bordering Lake Jericho. She noticed an animal that appeared to her to be a full-grown mountain lion in a lot where here livestock and deer gather at a salt block. She described what she saw as a very large brownish cat with a long tail. It was standing on the bed of a farm wagon. She saw it as she approached the feed lot when she was only 40 to 50 feet away. The day before, a dead deer had been discovered in the same area, maybe 100 feet away from the spot where she saw the mountain lion.

Again, wildlife officials say there is no evidence that a large cat is roaming the area. That doesn't stop the reports that keep rolling in.

"We're getting swamped with phone calls. I'm getting phone calls at home at night. I've had people show up here (at the office) wanting to know if something escaped from me. That answer is NO!" said Barbara Rosenman, who was at the time Director of Kentucky Wildlife Line Incorporated. This organization is a non-profit wildlife preserve in Oldham County.

One official privately conceded to Mr. Crawford, "They're here, and they've been here for a long time!"

Solid evidence is still the missing factor to prove that mountain lions, cougars, puma, panther, catamount (or by many other names) inhabit this state with us. By nature, they are elusive animals, and if they are out there, they are avoiding us.

These big cats in their natural habitats are usually nocturnal, and hunt early in the day and at dusk. If there are such animals present in Kentucky, they are probably the result of animals that have been exotic animals kept illegally as pets and then released.

Ms. Rosenman pointed out to Bryon Crawford that if these reported animals have been raised in captivity and then released, they would not have the same natural fear of humans as those spending their lives in the wild. Someone would more than likely see them rummaging through garbage, or raiding pet food sources. She noted that Michigan has confirmed population of Eastern Cougars.

Lisa Quire, a medical assistant, who lives in the Rose Hill Estates in the Little Kentucky River in Henry County had a thought provoking story. She believes it was a mountain lion that killed her pet Pit bull on a spring morning.

The dog was a house pet and described as "non-aggressive." When Ms. Quire left for work, she left the dog securely tied in the back yard, knowing her family would bring him back in when they got up. To their shock, the dog was found almost dead and lying on the side porch. The dog's wounds included bites and puncture wounds all over his head and throat. He had cat scratches on his hind quarters that were lined about an inch apart.

When Ms. Quire took the dog to the vet, she was told that another dog could not have caused that type of injuries. They were perhaps from a large bobcat or even something bigger.

When Ms. Quire called to report the attack to the Henry County Conservation officer, Toney Rucker, she was told that in the previous two weeks, there had already been about 30 calls from the Pendleton area about a large cat.

Lieutenant Frank Floyd of Trimble County and Sargent Glenn Watson of Oldham County, who are both Kentucky Fish and Wildlife officers, said they and biologists with the department have so far been unable to find any evidence that proved a mountain lion may have been responsible for the recent losses of pets and small livestock.

Another story from Bryon Crawford is from Jason and Tassy Smith who have a very large Trimble County family farm near the Little Kentucky River between Bedford and Cambellsburg. They lost a two-day old colt to an unidentified predator one night. They were unaware of the mountain lion reports, so assumed the new colt was perfectly safe.

Unfortunately, they did not think to check the horse lot for tracks after they found the dead colt. Tassy Smith said it looked as if a large animal had tried to drag the colt under an electric fence.

There have been unconfirmed sightings of big cats near the river bluffs in Henry County for many years, but again, no one has been able to produce satisfactory evidence to prove that big cats roam there.

Mr. Crawford's contacts across the state are far reaching. In a conversation with Harry Caudill (author of *Night Comes to the Cumberlands*), Mr. Caudill told him that he had absolutely seen a mountain lion along the Little Shepherd Trail. He also said that a Corp of Engineers employee had seen one.

The Conservation officer in Letcher County told Mr. Crawford about a group of people that had just come outside of their church after service one Sunday and saw a tawny colored mountain lion in the church yard. There were a number of people in that group who saw it.

"Even though these stories were researched and incorporated over a number of years while I was writing for the *Courier Journal*, they still have a good shelf life," said Mr. Crawford.

Malcolm (https://commons.wikimedia.org/wiki/File:Cougar.jpg)Cougar", black and white by user, https://creativecommons.org/licenses/by-sa/2.5/legalcode

Who's Watching Whom?

By Ernest Solar

Christine (my girlfriend at the time, my wife now) and I were camping at Abram's Creek Retreat and Campground in Elk Garden, West Virginia. Our tent site was by the creek that ran through the campground. It was a nice site. Facing the tent, to the right was the creek, to the left a steep hill. Behind the tent were several large boulders that lead up the steep hill. Behind us was the picnic table and fire pit. The ground was damp from an earlier rain, but not saturated.

We ate dinner for the night, and then built a fire. We burned some Native American incense in the fire. We talked and read into the night.

Approximately 9 pm, we put the fire out and retired to our tent. I am a heavy sleeper, which frustrates Christine when we are camping (well, anytime really). She is a light sleeper and usually hears things that I miss.

When she hears something, she wakes me and asks, "What was that?" I usually don't know because I didn't hear it. If I did "think" I heard something I usually give a response that only adds to her frustration. On this particular night she smelled something around 1:00 or 2:00 a.m. in the morning.

Christine woke me and said that she smelled something awful. I didn't smell anything. She was afraid that the outhouse at the top of the hill had overflowed and was running down past our tent. She wanted me to check. So, both of us got out of the tent, turned on the flashlight and looked around. There was no overflow from the outhouse.

Christine commented that she needed to use the restroom. So, we climbed the hill via a small single-track trail and walked about two hundred yards or so to the outhouse. As she relieved herself I stared at the moon. We then walked back down to our tent, down the trail.

When we reached our camp site I used the flashlight to look around the picnic table, cooler, and bag of trash to see if anything was disturbed. Nothing was out of place. I admit I looked for bigfoot tracks near our tent because awful, horrible smells have been associated with bigfoot and I thought maybe one passed our tent. We saw no tracks.

Christine and I stood facing our tent. I panned the flashlight about chest height (I'm 5'11", so about 5 feet off the ground) from right to left behind our tent. As the light passed through the trees lining the creek and then over the boulders we both saw what looked like a white mountain lion/panther sitting on its back haunches looking at us. We hadn't seen it, but it was sitting there watching us. As the light passed over the big cat, I quickly swung the beam of light back toward the creature. We saw it again in the same position.

Neither of us remembers seeing any eye shine. The creature was only illuminated for a second before it turned to our left and slowly sauntered up the pile of large boulders and the hill behind our tent and out of sight. I followed the mountain lion with the beam of light until it disappeared into the bushes and trees on the hill. We both remember seeing and commenting on how long and bushy the tail was.

I scanned the area one more time with the flashlight and then we got into our tent. We discussed what we saw and then fell asleep. We did not hear any sounds before or after the event. In the morning, we looked for prints, but found nothing.

I don't remember precisely the date that this happened, but it would have been early spring of 2011. I would say during the first half of spring break, so probably late March. It happened after midnight, closer to 1:00 or 2:00 a.m. in the morning. There was a full or almost full moon that night. However, where our tent was we were under thick tree canopy cover. I remember the moon because I was staring at it while Christine was using the outhouse.

This took place at Abram's Creek Retreat and Campground in Elk Garden, West Virginia.

In all honesty, it felt like the mountain lion was watching us, as if the creature was curious about us. Because of the white color of the creature we felt the creature was a spirit animal. We thought maybe we had somehow summoned a spirit creature by burning the Native American incense. At the time it never occurred to us that it could have been albino. We never felt like we were in danger. We felt the experience was more of a gift than anything else.

I will share a little bit about us. At the time of the sighting, my wife was a nanny for a family with three kids. I was a high school special education teacher working with students with emotional disabilities.

Currently, my wife is a stay-at-home mom and I am a professor of special education at a small liberal arts college. At the time of the event and currently my wife and I are both avid hikers. Christine is from Northwest Pennsylvania and grew up in the woods. I am from Northern Virginia, but started hiking, especially the Appalachian Trail, at an early age. Growing up I spent a lot of time in the mountains of West Virginia visiting family.

Over the past ten years my wife and I have backpacked up and down the east coast, New Mexico, Colorado, Montana, and Washington state. Our most enjoyable backpacking trip was hiking across Scotland back in 2015.

Currently, we live in an environmentally friendly neighborhood surrounded by 90 acres of woodland that connects with the C & O Canal, Appalachian Trail, and the Potomac River. It is safe to say that we walk in the woods on a daily basis.

We are not hunters. We do not have a problem with hunting. We chose not to hunt for a specific reason. We believe that nature and animals can feel our intention. We believe nature and animals can feel everyone's intention as they step into the forest.

Our intention is to explore, to wander, to wonder, to be a part of their world. We believe the experiences we have had is because of our intention. We feel that if we hunt we would corrupt the intention of being one with nature.

1896 Black Panther Engraving

Grandma's Black Panther

By Sheila Roberson

I just got off the phone with my momma and according to her and her sister this is an incident that happened to my grandmother. Grandma was around twelve years old at the time of the sighting, so this was back in 1920s or there about.

Grandma and her siblings were playing in the woods of Roane County, West Virginia when they spotted a black panther. They immediately left the area and headed home. They told their parents what they had seen.

Her father (my great grandfather), went looking to see if the big cat was still around. He discovered tracks near their home and believed the panther had followed them home.

I remember my grandma telling the story to us as we were growing up. She was a great cat lover.

Vintage Public Domain Image

View from the Porch

By Megan Minish

It was early summer in 2007. I was at my sister's house on Avery's Creek Rd in Arden, North Carolina. It was dusk, and she and I were standing on the front porch having an after-dinner cigarette.

Directly across the road from us was a cow field. The cows had already wandered off to a different part of the field that wasn't visible to us, so it was quite empty. There was a nice view of the mountain behind the field in the distance and in the pink and lavender light it made for a very pretty picture.

Suddenly, I noticed movement out of the corner of my left eye. I looked toward the left end of the field and saw a dark, solid shadow slinking past. It was a black panther! It wasn't running, but was moving quickly, crouched low to the ground, with its tail straight out behind it.

The cat was enormous. As long as a man, it was, with a tail nearly as long as the panther itself. We had a clear view of it from where we were standing. The porch was tall. We were on a hill and the field was very, very close. We had a good ten seconds worth of watching it cross the field and then it disappeared into the trees on the other side.

Afterwards, my sister and I just kind of looked at each other with open mouths. Later we would both agree that it was a moment in life when you're very glad that someone else was there to see the same thing you did. Even if nobody else ever believes us, we both know what we saw that evening and what we saw was a real, live, black panther.

Marshall County, West Virginia

By Kerry Merinar Colbert

I grew up in rural Marshall County in West Virginia. There have been sightings dating back to the 60s of mountain lions. They have been seen and heard in and around our farm and neighboring farms.

If yellow does exist, why can't the black ones? Years back one was shot in the southern part of our county and it had an Illinois game tag in its ear. I saw the pictures.

Vintage Public Domain Image

Influenced by a Sighting

By Sheila Roberson

My story happened on New Year's Eve of 1989 in MacClenny, Florida. I was supervisor of an industrial floor cleaning company called 'Dust Busters' and had serviced the floors of the MacClenny Food Lion that night.

It was right at midnight and it was raining lightly. I was on Hwy 301 heading back to base in Yulee, Florida. I had to cross over on an overpass. When I was close to the bottom my headlights caught the black panther and it turned and looked in my direction.

I wasn't going fast and came to a complete stop. There was no other traffic out, so I just stayed there for a long time (it seemed like) looking at the panther. The eyes of the panther reflected back an amber color in the headlights. The cat wasn't very large. It maybe weighed 40 - 50 pounds and its tail was as long as it's body.

There is no doubt in my mind as to it being black and being a cougar/puma/ Florida panther.

It wasn't scary, and I didn't take it as a bad omen (black cat crossing path). I felt blessed to see such a magnificent creature.

No one believed me, so I stopped telling people.

I have run private animal rescues for the past 15+ years, and black cats and feral cats are my focus. I don't know if my encounter influenced me, but it has left a powerful love for those that are harder to adopt. My current rescue is *Gargoyles Animal Rescue* and I have eight black cats in my care.

CCO – Creative Commons Public Domain – no attribution required

Randolf County, West Virginia

By Rocky Watson

Two years ago in lower Glady in Randolph County, West Virginia, my husband saw a panther standing in the little dirt road. He was in his truck. He watched it a couple of minutes before it went over the bank.

Somerset, Kentucky

By Charity Terlecky Bowker

I saw one while I was driving last year in Somerset, Kentucky, around that area. I'm not sure what the road name or number was, as I'm not from there. It was looking down a cliffside at the traffic.

It was an amazing animal. There was such a long tail on that cat! I'll never forget that moment.

Daniel Boone National Forest

By Susie White

There are black panthers in the Daniel Boone National Forest in Kentucky. My dad has told me of seeing them, and so has my ex-husband.

Cohutta Wilderness

By George Brewer, Jr.

I saw one in northwest Georgia on Highway 411 just south of the Tennessee line down into Georgia. It happened about three years ago in broad daylight. My sighting was at the edge of the Cohutta Wilderness Area.

No Doubts

By Rachel Hudson

All of the doubts people express about the existence of black panthers is so funny to me. I know my animals. I also know the "silent runners" as my Aunt calls them. She lived close to what they called "Painter Hollar."

I also know the difference between a cat and a bobcat. The black panthers are jet black without any spots or splotches.

By the Apple Tree

By Wille Lou Grasher

I walked out of our back door and saw a panther. It was asleep by the apple tree next to the outhouse. That was in 1965 in Harlan, Kentucky.

Forsyth County, North Carolina

By Georgia Holley

My mother's family lived on a large piece of land that backed up to the woods in Forsyth County, North Carolina. This incident happened in the early 1970s.

When my mom was little (around eight or nine years old), her mother told her to go hang out the clean clothes. She went outside after her mom left to hang the clothes out on the line, as she had been told.

She saw something out of the corer of her eye. She looked up to see what it was, thinking it would be a deer or something, but it was a panther. She froze, and it slowly turned around and went back into the woods.

She dropped the clothes and went back inside. She didn't finishing hanging up the washing on the line as she had been told. She was too afraid to go back out until grandma got home.

My grandma thought she told that whole story just to get out of hanging out the clothes, but she still says a panther is what she saw. She never saw it again.

Mistaken Identity?

By Jeremy D. Wells

I saw what I would have sworn was a big black cat, stalking through a field once. Because it was a Saturday, and there was no traffic, I was able to stop, back up, and really watch.

Eventually I saw a big black dog poke his head up over the grass. But, the way he had stalked and pounced, I'd have initially sworn he was a big black cat.

It's interesting how easy it is to misidentify something, especially when you can't get a good, clear look.

I've had several folks tell me that they have seen big black cats, but none have provided photos or videos. I HAVE seen photos and video of tawny colored big cats.

Now, Kentucky DNR claims there are no mountain lions here, despite those videos and photos. They claim those photos are of escaped or released exotic pets. That might be debatable. But even in places where we know there are mountain lions, melanistic (black) lions have never been documented.

I'm interested in the stories either way, and why folks believe what they saw was a "black cat." But, according to science, any black cat that was seen isn't a mountain lion.

(Maybe folks are seeing tawny ones at night and it just looks black because of lighting? Maybe folks are seeing dogs? Maybe they are seeing escaped/released exotics? Maybe there is some completely unknown cat out there, or a known wild cat outside its known range?)

But regardless of what is going on, folks keep reporting them.

Screamers

By Albert Shell

I've heard them scream in Carter County, Tennessee on the other side of beautiful Roan Mountain.

Wayne County, Kentucky

By Elaine NBobby Philpot

I saw a black panther in Wayne County, Kentucky years ago.

Clay County, West Virginia

By Vicky Jarrett

I saw one in Clay County, West Virginia several years go. She climbed up the side of a tree and screamed at me. I screamed also! I was scared to death!

We both ran in opposite directions.

Barbour County, West Virginia

By Christina Reger

A black panther was seen in Barbour County, West Virginia two years ago.

Riverdale, Georgia

By Steven Pittman

I saw one back in the 1950s off Highway 138 outside Riverdale, Georgia. I was a kid and it scared me half to death. It was black.

Behind My House

By Sharon Morgan Shepherd

We have a panther living up on the mountain behind my house. We think it is the same one that has been seen several times.

My granddaughter saw it jump into the road coming from the highway. It stopped and looked at her and off up the side of the mountain it went. The hunting dogs went into their doghouse and never made a sound.

My grandson was riding his four-wheeler around the hill from the house one day. The panther jumped up onto the road and straight up the hill in front of him.

A friend visiting my daughter. She came out of the house to get into her car. There was a panther sitting behind her car. When it heard her, it raised up. When it saw her, it ran up the mountain.

It is kind of scary knowing that the big cat lives so close and is not afraid to be seen. They are fast and can disappear really fast.

A Panther Scream

By Austin Price

I'm from Franklin, North Carolina. I lived on Cowee Mountain when this happened.

One evening we heard what sounded like a woman screaming like she was getting beaten. It sounded like it was coming from somewhere behind the house. We ran out in the yard and looked behind the house, trying to find where the sound was coming from.

We heard it again and looked up the hill. There she was. She took off and turned into a briar thicket, but we could see perfectly what she was.

Southwest Virginia

By Shelby Jean Payne Maxwell

I live in Southwest Virginia. I have seen a yellow panther up close. I even saw it snatch a bird out of the nest. When I tell this story, some believe it and some don't.

My nephew saw a black one in a field on his way to work in Tennessee.

Magnificent Creature

By Marcia Gabbard

I've seen a black panther in southeast Kentucky. It was the most magnificent creature I've ever laid eyes on. It had huge green eyes.

I saw it near a river on my way home from work around 1:00 am.

No one believes me, of course, but I don't care. I know what I saw and feel very privileged to have seen one.

Night Screamer

By Sherry Bowman

I have never seen one, but have heard one. It was over in Buchanan County, up the holler. It sounded like a woman screaming.

My kids and I were up late watching TV. Their daddy was working at the mines. Those screams scared us all, but I went outside because I thought it was the neighbors cscreaming. It was not.

The children and all of the adults who heard it still talk about it. It must have been passing through. It was there for about a week, screaming every night. It was something I'll never forget.

Panther Encounters

By Tony Felosi

My first panther encounter was approximately in 1983 in Mary Helen, Kentucky. It happened on top of a mountain that I was working on. I was driving a truck, hauling coal. I was going to a coal washer early on a late fall morning, maybe around 5:00 or 5:30. It was still dark.

On the way to the shop, a big cat barrels out of the woods, close to the bank. It leapt into the middle of the road. The tail was as long was the cat was! It was a dun colored one, sort of a cream color. When he jumped into the road, he kind of glanced me, then bounded out of the road. So, to be perfectly clear, he jumped off the bank and landed in the middle of the road with one jump, then looked at me and jumped again, going completely across the rest of the road and over the bank.

I would estimate the animal to have weighed about 150 pounds, maybe a little more. It was very large for a cat around here. I've seen maybe fifty bobcats over the years, but never anything like the size of that cat.

That was my first sighting. My second sighting was on the same mountain range, but on the opposite side, close to Chevrolet Hollow. As the crow flies, the encounters took place about six or seven miles from my initial sighting.

The second one happened in the evening about two years later in summer. I was coming from a truck shop on that side of the mountain where we hauled the coal to two washers on top of the mountain, the Wallace and the Mosley. I was coming from the Mosley Washer about three miles back to our other truck shop. The coal was washed on top of the mountain, then belted to the bottom.

As I was heading from one truck shop to the other, just about the same thing happened. The exception was that this cat stayed in the road just a little longer than the first time I saw one.

A black panther jumped into the road ahead of the truck and just stopped there and stared at me. I stopped the truck and stared at the big cat. It was very unusual. I was looking at it and it was looking at me.

The thought hit me that I probably needed to put the vehicle in reverse and get out of there. It wasn't aggressive or anything. It was very unusual to have a black panther jump out in front of a truck and just stand there in the middle of the road staring at me. Apparently, it decided it was time to move on, looked away, and leaped across the rest of the road in one big jump. It was covering probably fifteen feet per jump, effortlessly.

Seeing a big cat like that will surely take you by surprise. Seeing it's power in the ability to leap and cover so much ground that easily makes a huge impression.

I've been in and around the woods all of my life. I've seen bear, turkey, bobcats, and you name it, but those are the only two big cats in the wild that I've ever seen up close.

Bobcats are not that uncommon. I've seen plenty of them. I've seen them at different times when I was hunting, hiking, or four-wheeling. They follow the game trails.

It is easiest to see any animal in the forest after a fresh snow that has covered the ground for two or three days when they are looking for food. They start moving around more, trying to find something to eat.

I've actually had them walk by my truck and be that bold. I mean literally walk beside of the truck, look up at me, and then keep going.

Walking the Dogs

By Sandra Smith

My husband was walking the dogs toward the back of our property. We live on thirty acres. The big cat was lying under a tree, sleeping. T and the dogs saw it and STOPPED!

T said, "The cat got up, stretched, and turned. It walked back into the woods."

He and the dogs walked (quickly) to the neighbors' house. Their house backed up to our property.

He said, "That cat had the longest tail I've ever seen. It scared the livin' crap out of me!"

No one has seen it since, but we hear it all the time!

Interstate 79

By Pat Heater

We have both yellow mountain lions and black panther in West Virginia. I have seen a yellow one near my home just a few months ago. A black one crossed the I-79 in front of my car!

Bailey's Creek Road

By Nancy Middleton

I saw one on Bailey's Creek Road around 2011 at 4:00 in the afternoon in Evarts, Kentucky. I was driving up the road and it jumped out of the woods and ran across the road and disappeared into the woods on the other side of the road about as fast as I could tell my cousin, "Look! Look! Look!"

Then three turkeys came out of the woods. I think the cat had left. It was probably stalking the turkeys and I disturbed them. I had no time to grab the camera and I didn't even think to look for tracks.

I kept telling my cousin, "Roll up that window! Roll it up!" I was afraid that big cat might jump in through the car window!

I had a 150 pound dog at the time and that cat was bigger than my dog!

My cousin saw it also, but we have no proof at all except our eye witness accounts.

Cutting House

By Linda Berry

When my husband Robert was a young man in the 60s, he lived in Middle Fork area near Rosman, North Carolina. His dad was a butcher and had set aside a cutting room out behind his garage.

On numerous occasions they had unwanted visitors coming to their home right after his dad had butchered meat. Robert said that mountain lions smelled the raw meat and blood, so they tried to break into the cutting room. These were the big yellow or brown ones.

The Rabbit Chase

By Real Harris

I've got a story about seeing a black panther.

I was about 23 years old at the time, and I had a 76 Chevy square body. Anyway, it was about 2:00 a.m. in the morning when I pulled up to Dad's house like I always do. I was a little bit back from the woodshed when I parked.

I hopped out of my truck, slamming my door because it was an old truck. I walked around to the little front passenger side of my truck when I stopped for a moment.

At this time, a rabbit ran out of the dark next to my wood shed, and ran out in front of me, and dodged over the bank. At that same time a black panther ran out from my wood shed after the rabbit and made a 90-degree turn when the rabbit went over to bank.

The black panther did not follow the rabbit. It made that quick turn and went up a main trail we had cut out through the woods. The scary part was when I had to continue my walk up the hill and into the house!

Believe me or not, it's up to you. The game warden says they are not here, but when you see one, you know they are here.

Three Encounters

By Vonda and Glenn Marlow

I lived on Watts Creek, Kentucky in 1987 in a house up on the side of the hill. I used to walk outside on the porch at night and smoke.

One night I walked out on the porch for a cigarette and heard the awfulest noise! What it sounded like to me was a woman screaming.

I ran back in the house and told my husband Glenn that it sounded like someone was killing a woman. We stood outside for a little while and listened. We kept on hearing the sound. It was the most awful screams that I have heard in my life. The hair stood straight up on the back of my neck.

I was so afraid to walk outside in the night time again. Glenn said that he had heard them a few times living on the creek before we were married. When I shared this story with other people on the creek and they told me that it was panthers.

As kids, Dad and Mom would always take my brothers and me out on these old mining roads and target practice with Dad's pistol or his .22 rifle. We did this often.

One day we went up a road and looked down to see what was below us. There was a panther standing there looking at us. I know that we stood there over five minutes just standing real still looking at it.

It wasn't fat or anything. It was real skinny. I remember how coal black it was and that it had a real long black tail. All I was thinking was that it was going to come running at us and attack.

It was so beautiful!

As a teenager, I lived up at Closplint, Kentucky. Up the road a little way from where we lived was Sieber's Grocery. Word had spread fast that there was a baby bobcat under the back of the store and that some teenage boys had it hemmed up.

Here we all went up there and sure enough it was about four feet under the store. It was all backed up growling at us. I remember one of the boys had dared me to reach back under there and pull it out. Everybody laughed but me.

It was maybe about two feet long. I can still see its pretty eyes and can still remember that growling or meowing is what I called it.

Glenn said that his Mom told him one time that her Mom (his grandmother) had told a tale about a panther. She said that someone that she had known had given birth to a baby in the house. A panther was outside trying to tear the side of the house off to get in to that mother and her new baby.

People would always say that you had to watch when a new mother had a baby because the panthers would think that the little baby crying inside the house would be their cub. So, the panther would try to come in people's houses to get the babies.

Definitely NOT a Dog

By Kaitlyn Hensley

This incident took place in March of 2016 on Pine Mountain, Kentucky. I had ridden the four-wheeler out to my aunt's house. I got off of the four-wheeler and was gathering my stuff up to take in. When I looked up the road I saw a black figure hunkered down in the shadows of a pole light.

I thought to myself "that's a BIG dog."

It kept staring at me and I could feel it look me in the eyes. Finally, it got up and ran across the road over into the woods. As soon as it stood up, I realized it was not a dog. I saw the tail of the cat and that said it all.

I turned and ran through my aunt's driveway to get away from there. That was the most scared I've been in my life!

Public Domain CCO Image by David Raju Black Panther, melanistic Panthera pardus, at Nagarhole National Park, India

Shields, Kentucky

By April and Chris Payne

It was a cold winter morning. My husband and I were outside feeding our new puppy, Patches. As we were feeding her, I glanced up and saw a long black tail dangling from a tree branch.

At first, I was in disbelief and said to my hubby, "There is a black snake hanging from that tree!"

Chris looked further up in the tree. "That's a black panther!"

We quickly gathered Patches and her dog food and went back inside. After this incident, I decided to feed her inside the house and keep her in for a while. I was afraid she would get attacked by the panther. We decided we should continue to feed her inside and let her in and out.

Meanwhile, we always keep an eye open for the panther!

One bright early morning, we were working out in th yard taking care of our flowers and weeding the flowerbed. On the back side of our house is a mountain.

As we were in the front yard working away, we heard a peculiar noise. I said, "Did you hear that?"

My husband said, "Yes, I did!"

I asked him, "Is that a hurt cow?"

Chris said, "No! That is an elk!"

We looked behind the house in the back yard, and a huge elk rose up out of the cudzu vine! It was eating the vines!

I love living up here on top of a mountain. We love seeing all the wildlife and natural beauty.

As for the panther, we know it's out there, and we always pay attention to what's around us when we are outside.

I've Seen the Tracks of a Big Cat

By Jeremy Coffie

I haven't seen one myself, but my cousin swears up and down that he and his wife had a black panther cross the road in front of them while they were driving.

I do a lot of trapping here in Bell County, Kentucky and I know tracks pretty dang good. I have seen lion tracks in an area a few times now, but the warden says we don't have any kind of mountain lion here. Yet, one was killed around Lexington last season. I believe it was a yellow one.

Pike County, Kentucky

By David Coleman

I saw a yellow colored mountain lion in Pike County, Kentucky. It definitely was a mountain lion.

Root Digging

By Alisha Switzer Cooper

I am an avid root digger in north eastern Kentucky, in Lewis county. When I was out digging one day I came up on a panther. It sprinted off so fast, all I could see was a long black body going by.

When they scream it sounds like a woman being murdered. The sound is creepy. My grandfather had an encounter long ago, in the same general area.

Water Valley Road Sighting

By Betty Davis

I saw a black panther myself en route to work years back. It crossed the road right in front of me.

I was driving on Water Valley Road in southern Illinois when it happened.

The Chicken House Encounter

By Tammy Vandiver Adams

We live in the northern Georgia mountains. In the 1950s, before I was born, my mother went out to the chicken house to check on things. The chicken house was up on a hill behind our home.

When she topped the hill, there, lying in the morning sun right in front of the chicken house was a huge panther! Mama said it was a dark color, but with the sun shining on its coat, she could see a pattern underneath the dark.

Its long tail was twitching. Mama was afraid to turn around. She was afraid it would jump on her back. So, she walked backwards, back down the hill, and back to the house. When she got inside, she called my Grandpa who lived right out the road.

By the time he got to our house with his gun, the panther was gone. Grandpa called them "wompus cats."

Just a few years ago, my daughter saw one in the laurel thickets also. It was in the same area as the other one.

Three Point Panther

By Bert Noe

This is a story always told in our family. My uncle, Steve Smith, had been out with his buddies one night on a week-end spree. On the way home, they didn't want to drive him all the way to the place he was boarding with his uncle, Grant Noe, on my daddy's side. He was boarding with them while he worked in the coal mines. So, they let him off at the mouth of the holler at Three Point.

There were no street lights to brighten his way home. He had total darkness except for star light. A couple of houses sat on the hillsides when he first started walking up that way, but they had gone to bed early, and all of their lights were out. His only choice was to keep hoofing it in the blackness.

He had a couple of miles to go when he started hearing a blood curdling sound like a woman screaming. He was sure it was a panther based on the volume of the sound, louder than a bobcat or other ordinary cat. It was staying right with him, screaming every once in a while.

His nerves got the best of him and he decided it was time to run for it and hope the cat didn't get him. When he got to the house, he jumped the porch and hit the front door full force.

He took the door down, hinges and all! He was too scared to take time to knock or scream.

Panther Screams

By Verla Lynn Lewis

When I was a little girl, we lived at Blair, above Cumberland, Kentucky. It was near where Brock's church is now. The panthers would be all around our house at night. They would get on top of a building in front of our house. I can still hear their screams. I was always so scared of them!

Neighbor's Driveway

By Haley Blackburn

When I was younger, my brother and I were playing outside and heard a weird noise. Naturally we ran inside. A few moments later, Mom looked out the window and saw a panther walking across our neighbor's driveway in Northeast, Georgia.

Ohio

By Dennis Nally

I have a friend who swears on his mom's grave that he saw one here in Ohio.

Panther in East Tennessee

By Regina Headden

We have panthers here, too, in the East Tennessee mountains. Oakdale is a small rural town where seeing a variety of wild animals is the norm. My dad grew up in Oakdale and worked hard to get his railroad job in Atlanta transferred to his hometown.

We moved to Oakdale in July of 1969. Within the first two months of living here, my dad saw a bear, and it left signs that it was around for about three or four years. On his way to work one day, Dad nearly hit a bobcat running down the middle of the road. It wasn't unusual to see wild turkeys, deer, and an occasional fox.

However, the scariest of the wild animals that several of my family members encountered was the black panther.

Dad was working the night shift on the railroad in late summer around 1971. He was walking in the railroad yards inspecting train cars when he noticed a rustling sound in the foliage between the rails and the banks of the Emory River that ran parallel to the tracks. Needless to say, his pace picked up and the rustling continued.

When he reached the other end of the train where his co-worker was sitting in their truck, he jumped in and quickly closed the door. He told his co-worker what had happened, and they decided to drive slowly back to the yard office to see if they could tell what was following Dad up the tracks.

They didn't have to look very long. As the co-worker pulled the truck around on the access road, the headlights caught a glimpse of a huge black cat-like animal staring at them. They knew it was a panther. From that point on, they made sure the rest of their co-workers were careful when working at night in the north yards.

For a while, there were tales about black panthers being seen throughout the surrounding communities of Oakdale. My family never had another encounter with a panther until one summer night in the late 1980s (probably 1988 or 89). My two younger sisters worked the evening shift in the next town over the mountain. They usually got home between 11:30 and midnight. We always used the back door to enter and leave our house, and Mom made sure the porch light was on so my sisters could see to get in the door.

As my sisters rounded the corner of the house to get to the back door, they both saw it at the same time. A huge black panther was sitting between them and the door. They screamed, and thankfully the panther quickly disappeared up the mountain behind the house. Mom heard the screams, and everyone in the house was awakened as my sisters pushed each other through the door still screaming.

Of course, Dad had to go investigate, but he only heard a distant rustling of the kudzu up the mountain.

Years would go by, and we did not see any sign of a panther around the house. However, I believe it returned in 2003 even though I did not see it. My dad died in an accident at our house on May,19 of that year. That same night, we learned that Mom had a serious health problem that could be fatal.

Mom was in the hospital for over three weeks, so I was home by myself during that time. At least twice during that time I was awakened by a huge thud on the roof above my bedroom. The thud was followed by the sound of something scraping as it slid across the roof and eventually jumped from the roof. I could not see anything, but in my mind, I knew it was a panther.

We still relive these stories every now and then as we remember the 34 years of living in Oakdale.

I Know What I Saw

By Randy Feltner

Being born and raised in southeast Kentucky has given me a lifetime of opportunities to see all kinds of wildlife. But, one animal really stands out as a once in a lifetime experience.

It was midsummer 2008 and I had gathered with a group of friends and family to ride four-wheelers in an area of Perry County, Kentucky named Viper. One other person besides myself witnessed the cat.

We were leading the group along a trail on Right Fork Maces Creek. It was a beautiful but hot day. We rounded a bend in the trail and I caught movement in the tree line ahead of us about 50 yards.

Like a scene out of a movie, a huge black cat jumped from the tree line and landed in the middle of the trail. Another jump and it was gone!

My friend and I stopped, and he asked, "Was that what I think it was?"

There's no doubt what we saw. A black cat, (panther, puma, mountain lion???) It was close in size to a German shepherd dog and cleared a thirty-foot wide trail in one bounce.

Two years later during spring turkey season in the nearby town of Vicco, a lifelong friend witnessed a black cat roughly the same size. He watched it stalk a flock of turkey for nearly fifteen minutes until the birds spooked and the cat vanished.

We both have been laughed at, shrugged off, and called liars plenty of times when we talk about it to others. Most people think you're crazy or making up tall tales. But, I know what I saw, and I don't believe for one minute that my buddy would make up something as unusual as this, either.

I visited my grandparents shortly after our ride. When papaw heard my story he just grinned a little bit and in a hushed voice said, "You better watch who you tell because if the wrong people catch wind of a big black cat roaming around on the strip job, most likely someone would try to kill it."

He shared a few stories with me that evening of when he saw a black cat in the same general area several times back in the fifties.

I don't think the public has anything to worry about with these cats. They are beautiful animals that seem almost supernatural. I can still picture that slick black fur shimmering in the sunlight as it jumped across that road just like it was yesterday.

The Panther Watching Our Son

By Rhonda Arrowood

I live at River, Kentucky in Johnson County, just outside of Paintsville.

I've seen a black panther on two different occasions. The first time, I saw one was when my son was playing basketball on the court in our yard. He was nine years old.

He ran in the house and told me, "There's a big black panther sitting on a big rock watching me."

Oh, my gosh! We thought he was just being silly. We told him, "Get back out there and play!" We had no clue there really was something out there.

He did as we told him and went back outside. His dad went to the window to check on him. He ran to the door and told our son, "Walk slowly back to the house..."

He did, and the big cat sat there on the rock watching him. It was a big black panther. It had the biggest tail I'd ever seen!

After that, we watched for it, but we never saw it again.

About ten years after that, my son was working, and I would go and pick him up when he got off from work. It was about 3:00 in the morning and we were on our way back home after I had picked him up.

We had to drive past a farm that has horses. Walking along the fence line beside of the farm was a big black panther.

They are beautiful animals, but scary!

Image from Creative Commons Public Domain, Julie Langford, November 19, 2006

Caught in the Headlights

By Linda Berry

My husband and I lived in the Penrose Community of Brevard, North Carolina area. One night back in 1975 we were traveling on Ross Road close to the dog pound when we saw a huge black panther. Some call them pumas or mountain lions. It was sitting beside the highway, very close.

It was hypnotized by our head lights. As we drove by I checked out his long teeth as he flashed them at us. His or her sharp pointed ears were alert and his slick coal black body sat eye level from my passenger side window.

Needless to say, he was on alert snarling at us as passed. I've never been so frightened of an animal from inside my car! As we left him behind I looked in the rear view and saw him spin around and leap off into a wooded area.

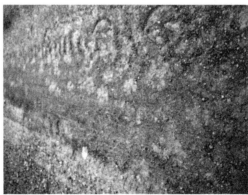

Photo by Judith Victoria Hensley

Black Panther Napping

By Melanie Richards

I had been cleaning in the house and decided to take a break and sit out on the porch with my dog, Max. I had a bag of trash to take out to the pen and Max escorted me hoping that maybe I'd take the time to play ball with him.

I got within about ten feet of the pen where I was going to put the trash bag. I was feeling about worn out from the day. I thought I'd save a few steps and toss the trash bag over into the pen instead of walking all the way up to it and dropping the bag in. I had been in poor health for a while, and the grass had gotten away from me around the edge of the yard. I had grown up enough so that when the bag went kerplop into the pen, it spooked a black panther that had been napping in the tall grass just beside of the pen.

It was not happy to have been startled at all! It took the stance that it was going to get me and my dog, but my dog ran over to it, as to say "Friends?" The big cat promptly slapped him around and he quickly ran back to me and hid behind my legs, so I was in between the both of them! I certainly had the thought that I was going to die that day!

I just stood there, staring at the green-eyed panther, waiting for it to take us both. Then it

sat down and just looked back at us, it's tail
swishing back and forth. It seemed like an
eternity standing there waiting for the
inevitable, but I figured that I might as well try
and say my piece before it happened.

I told it that if it didn't bother us, we
wouldn't bother it. It sat there for a little while
longer and then got up, looked around and
started easing over the bank that leads to the
woods by the creek. It seemed as though I had
been standing there for hours, but in reality, I
reckon it was only a few minutes. I was glad it
was gone.

About two weeks later, I heard growls from
behind the house while I was out in the front
yard, and then I heard a high pitched "screech"
sort of noise in the opposite direction. I got up
on the porch and sat down and just watched
and listened. I spotted what looked to be a black
house cat up on the hill, but with binoculars,
saw that it was a young panther! I tried to take
pictures of it, but they came out all blurry.

I hope this make some sense to you! This
was one of those life moments that happen and
there are no witnesses! I've seen many things
when I was back home, living by myself, on 115
acres in Hancock County, Kentucky. I was
always in the woods roaming around, I saw
a lot.

Panther Down the Chimney

By Charlene Bundy

My family lives at the head of a holler in Smith, Kentucky. When I was in kindergarten, my brother Brian was in the sixth grade. Our cousin, J. J. was in first grade. We all got off at the same bus stop and started walking on the road up the holler toward home.

There were some old cars sitting near our great grandparents' home place. There was a black panther sitting in the hood of one of those old cars. When it heard us kids running and laughing, it jumped. While it was in the air, its body was stretched out for the jump as long as the road was wide. It was jet back from nose to tail.

We were all very frightened and ran on home. We told Mamaw and Papaw. We told mom, but we knew it was long gone.

Papaw used to tell us about when he and his sisters were home alone one night. Mamaw and Papaw had gone to church, I think maybe to a funeral. He said the dogs were going crazy and suddenly a big black paw started swiping under the door. There was a big crack under the door and its paw fit under.

He said it let out a big scream that sounded like a woman screaming. His sisters were crying, and he grabbed a big butcher knife and stabbed the knife all the way through its paw and into the floor the next time it stuck it under the door. It jerked its paw a couple of times and broke free. They didn't see what happened to it, but it left the house and ran away.

Granny Opha used to tell about a man and a woman that had an experience with a panther way before she was born. They had built a little cabin at the foot of a big hill. The men would leave from time to time to get supplies. The young lady was pregnant.

When the man came home, he found her lying in her bed, dead. An animal had attacked her somehow and killed her.

He waited in the dark to see what had happened and how. Sometime during the night, he heard what he thought was a woman screaming. He waited and listened. Then he heard something hit the roof of the house.

Suddenly a big black panther came down the chimney. It had come back to eat on the woman's body. They didn't have dampers back then in the chimney and the panther came straight down the chimney, out into the cabin. The man shot and killed it.

It always bothered me when Granny told us this story. It was too graphic!

Shenandoah County

By Jesse Mathias

My mother was raised in Fort Valley, Shenandoah County, Virginia. She mentioned once that she heard what was believed to be a panther when she was a child. She said it sounded like a woman screaming, as if she was scared or hurt. That's the whole story as I remember it.

Outside of London, Kentucky

By Darrell Messer

The one I saw was in the Bush area outside of London, Kentucky. I was with my oldest brother. We both saw it. I've had others tell me they have seen one also in the Cold Hill area.

Panther Chasing Deer

By Laken Michelle

My encounter probably would have been in 2003. I was walking up my road around 11:00 p.m. with my sister and friends. I heard something in the field beside of where we were walking. I looked out in a field and saw this big black cat looking thing chasing deer. There were at least five deer. They ran and jumped the road in front of us. When the cat saw us, it turned around and in a matter of seconds disappeared into the darkness

Sunset Hunt – Free use by 4FreePhotos.com

Three Days of Screams

By Nancy Curtis

My encounter took place here in little ole Fall Branch, Tennessee. It happened about four years ago.

I thought our only neighbor was being murdered about at about 6:00 a.m. in the morning! I could hear the worst screams I had ever heard.

The direction of the "screams" kind of made a fairly large circle in the hills surrounding us. I put out some inquires and received some recordings. They were the same. It seemed there was a panther on the prowl, a mountain lion in heat, or whatever it was.

The screams continued and whatever kind of cat is was, it continued to prowl around for about three days that year. It returned about the same time the next year.

Since then there has been nothing but the hair-raising memories. That sound is something one never forgets!

A Black and Yellow Pair

By Jamie Couch

My wife, Christina, and I have been together for almost eight years and married six years this past February. Christina is an avid hunter. Every time I go, she is right on the back of my four-wheeler going with me. We have a four, soon to be five-year old little girl who is following step for step in our footsteps about loving the outdoors and hunting. Carlee Shawntae was hunting with us well before she was a year old.

Christina and I both kill out every season. We love to hunt together.

We were bow hunting one year in Letcher County, Kentucky. It was in the fall of the year and about an hour before dark. It was the first and last time since I was a young boy and started hunting that anything like this ever happened. One yellow cat like a mountain lion and one black cat (like what people would call a black panther) walked up on me and my wife Christina!

I don't know if it was a male and female pair, or what. We watched them for two hours! They were playing with each other and cutting up like two house cats, except we could clearly tell the difference in size. They were much bigger than house cats.

They never hurt each other. The only way to describe it was like they were playing together in the woods. We continued watching until it got dark and they wandered off.

They were the first and the last I have ever seen. I enjoy telling about our life together and our adventures.

If someone ever asks me, "Do you think panthers are real? Do you think they exist here in these mountains?" I can say beyond a shadow of doubt, "Yes, they exist!"

Britain Has Them, Too!

By Ashton Johnson

I've been told about sightings of mountain lions not far from my home. Black panthers are common in Britain, too, because of people releasing pets. But panthers are black jaguars. Mountain lions don't hold the gene for being melanistic.

Upsher County, Texas

By James Davis McCoy

Google "Black Panther sightings in Upshur County" for information on sightings and TV coverage in my native East Texas. There have been too many sightings in the past hundred years for it to be just a myth or someone mistaking a mountain lion for a black panther.

The legend of black panthers in East Texas is almost a supernatural phenomenon. Big cats are extremely elusive. Mostly, they see you, but you do not see them.

We live in Phoenix, Arizona and have a cabin in Crown King in the Bradshaw area where the mountain lion population is so high. Hunting them is part of state Game Management.

Black jaguars are indigenous to Northern Mexico, so why would they not venture into East Texas or Arizona? I've wondered if they could cross breed with a mountain lion?

* * * * *

I took James's advice and did a little research on the internet about black panther sightings in Upsher County. I recommend it to anyone who wants to pursue their own research.

From this link I also found a news cast report from WYFF News about a black panther sighting in the Greenville, Anderson, Spartanburg area of the Carolinas, near Paris Mountain. The woman in the interview from 2011 described a huge black cat visitor to her front porch. At least one other report on this same news channel has an official saying that there were several people reporting sightings of a big black creature roaming the area.

A report and video from Pennsylvania had been taken down and the video no longer available. This seemed to be the theme of things as I tried to check on headlines and videos. One from Louisiana had also been taken down and no longer available. There was also one from the Western Pennsylvania, Ohio border.

There is a YouTube video of a black panther in Arkansas. It is from a distance, but available for interested parties to view and draw their own conclusions. Another report is from Zanesville and Clark County by WDTNTV. There is a video showing tracks and a partially eaten carcass in a tree.

WLEX in Lexington, Kentucky also did a story based on reports of black panther sightings in the Lexington area. Typical of people's sightings, no matter how passionate they are about having seen what they believe is a black panther, officials from the Department of Fish and Wildlife simply say it is impossible, and that whatever they saw is not a black panther.

There is also footage on YouTube from West Virginia, but it did not look like a black panther in my opinion. It might have been a big black cat, but I didn't think it looked like a panther at all, except it was big and black.

There is footage of a black bobcat from West Virginia that is pretty awesome. It definitely has the shape, ears, and tail of a bobcat, but is solid black.

There are also fraudulent videos of black housecats that people are trying to pass off as black panthers. If you've ever seen one for real, these feeble attempts are frustrating, and might deceive someone who has not seen a black panther in real life.

A TWRA Tennessee news broadcast has footage of a cougar, and reports that they have at least six confirmed sightings of big tawny mountain lions that had not been seen in Tennessee for over 100 years. This is a 2016 report NC5, News at 10.

There are separate links to sightings in Kentucky, Illinois, Indiana, Georgia, Florida, Arkansas, Louisiana, North Carolina, Texas, and more. Happy web surfing!

- Judith Hensley

Berea, Kentucky

By Tammy Webb

I live in Madison County, Kentucky (Berea). I haven't seen a Cougar personally, but I have heard one! It was bone chilling. I can give you names of a couple of friends that did see one close to my home.

Panther on the Road

By Hollie Calloway

I saw a black panther about eleven years ago here in Mars Hill/Marshall, North Carolina. It was a huge beautiful creature with big yellow eyes.

I'll never forget the incident because we were almost face to face. I was in a car and it was right in middle of the road. We waited for it to move.

It wasn't scared of us a bit. It took its sweet time, and when we drove beside it slowly I got to see it up close. It was amazing!

The Bonfire

By Charlene Bundy

My family enjoys bonfires. We had one probably around six years ago that gave us all a surprise.

We were all just sitting around campfire talking and all of a sudden, an extremely loud big cat roared. We all stopped in our tracks and just stared at each other, not sure of what we had just heard. It was so loud, I thought it was right behind us.

My husband assured me that it was farther away than I thought, and the sound had carried from a farm just across the road. This location happens to be where my other friends saw a cougar.

When we got home that night, I googled large cat sounds. We listened to several that didn't match. But when I pulled up a recording for "cougar," it was a dead on match to the sound we all heard. It made the hair stand up on the back of your neck!

The Missing Cousin

By Jenny Justice

When my mother, Lillian Dickson, was in her teens just prior to World War I, her family lived in a very rural area in Hardin County, Tennessee. All travel was horse generated then, and all the young people rode horseback.

My mother's father's family was large. There were eight siblings, and there were many cousins of my mother's generation. There was no entertainment available except getting together in one home or another for parties to play cards or games. Travel to and from these parties was always by horseback, of course.

One night after a party at my mother's parents' house all the visitors headed homeward in different directions. The next morning my grandparents received word of a terrible tragedy. One of the cousins didn't arrive back home that night although his horse did. At first light the next morning his brother set out in search of him, hoping that the horse had just somehow unhitched itself from the post and that his brother was safely stranded with my grandparents.

This was not to be.

As the brother was traveling the path Aaron would have taken, he heard a weak cry for help. Quickly dismounting and securing his horse, he rushed to the sound of the cries. Aaron was severely injured and unable to move his legs, signaling a possibly severed spine, but even worse was a huge swelling on his forehead.

He told his brother he thought he was dying but tried to hold on until someone came along who could tell his parents what happened to him. He told his brother that a panther had jumped down in the path ahead of them and spooked the horse causing the horse to turn and run into the woods under an overhanging limb which caused the head injury and knocked him off the horse.

The brother wanted to leave immediately to fetch help, but Aaron begged him to stay with him, saying that he knew he was dying. He then became unconscious and died a few minutes later.

I was born in 1927, and the family frequently talked about it when I was a child

Taller than My Front Bumper

By Karen Booth Waldrop

I was travelling at night on Cross Mountain Road between Johnson and Carter Counties, Tennessee. It happened one night in 2005. A black panther ran across the road in front of me.

I had to slam on the brakes to keep from hitting it. I was driving a 1992 Chevrolet Blazer and it was a little taller than my front bumper.

God's Beautiful Creation

By Tommy Slaven

When I was a young boy in Eastern Kentucky we were sitting on the front porch one night and heard a big cat's scream on the hillside. It sounded like a woman screaming or a baby crying

I saw one on the Blue Ridge Parkway in Western North Carolina at night while I was driving. They are one of God's beautiful creations!

They're Still Here

By Linda Berry

When my mom was a young girl back in 30's, she lived in Brevard, North Carolina. Back then people were poor and struggling to survive. They had lived during the Great Depression.

Mom's dad logged puff wood for a living. My mom dropped out of school and she and her sister used a cross cut saw to fall the trees. As I was growing up mom spoke of her childhood often.

There was one particular story that always stuck with me.

One night, mom went outside to go to the bathroom. Back then they had out houses instead of indoor plumbing. On that particular night she decided to not to use the outhouse, preferring instead to stay close to her house. She was afraid to venture too far by herself.

Mom said that while she sat there a big black panther came up beside her and sat down next to her in the dark. She said it sat there staring at her. It was very intimidating. Luckily, she was able to escape into the house without injury.

There have been many such close encounters with mountain lions or panthers in our area, and the stories have been passed down through generations here. Panthers are still heard and seen here.

They're not afraid of women and children. I've heard they will attack females and young kids but they're somewhat intimated by men.

They're still here in the area. We use to live in a home bordering Pisgah National Forest. As a child mom told me if I ever heard a woman screaming in the woods not to go and try to find her. She said, "It's not a woman. It's a panther. They sound like a woman in great pain."

Little did I know would eventually hear one.

I was standing in our kitchen one evening when I heard a high-pitched blood curdling scream. I was paralyzed with fear. I ran to mom and ask what that was. She said, "Linda that's a panther screaming."

I'll never forget that sound

The Outhouse Panther

By Esther Boyd

I grew up in Alabama. When I was seven or eight years old, my family went to a little country church (in the wildwoods) I called it the Salem Holiness Church near Piedmont, Alabama.

It was just a little white frame church. It was very small. It had an old long wooden table outside to be used for "dinner on the ground" or Homecoming's. We didn't have an indoor bathroom and had an old outhouse on the edge of the woods out back.

We only had a small congregation, just a few families gathered there for services. A little older lady that attended the church (she will remain nameless) went out one evening to the outhouse at the night service by herself. We (my older sister Kay and my mother), always went out together. Momma always taught us to be careful.

The lady went out during the service and a few minutes later came running back in a frenzy, scared and crying. She said she opened up the outhouse door and came face to face with a black panther!

She was okay, except for being scared to death.

We had friends that lived in that little community and others talked of having seen big cats and hearing them too. This was talked about by my family many times, on many occasions.

Over the years others have spoken of many sightings of large cats (some different colors) in the Piedmont mountainous area, and also Dugger Mountain near Borden Springs in Alabama.

Vintage 1800 book plate print – public domain

Childhood Adventures

By Rene White

I grew up in a hollow called Barwick near Buckhorn State Park in Kentucky. The circle on the map is my parents' house.

The Star was the oldest part of the strip job at the time when this sighting occurred. The rest of the strip job was in the first stages of grow bac.

We used to go four-wheeling way back there when I was around ten. We would always see huge paw prints on the trail too big for anything other than a mountain lion.

There was an area that we called "the tip" because the area went to a point in a big holler full of cliffs and cavers. One day we were back there, and we heard something drop wet out of a tree. We, being dumb kids, went looking and found a half-eaten deer that had fallen out of the tree.

We saw the back end of a big cat running up the hill. We could clearly see that much, and that it had a long tail. Needless to say, we hightailed it out of there!

My best friend lives on that road there near The Star. A few weeks later, she came to me at school and told me that she and her dad almost hit a black panther with their truck.

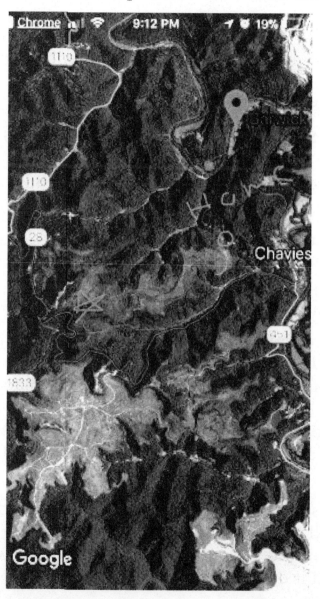

I knew then I wasn't crazy. She said from nose to tail, it was almost as long as the road was wide.

Now, it seems crazy to think of the distance our parents let us travel as kids. We had pellet guns and a radio on us in case of emergencies. That wouldn't have been much help with a mountain lion.

We also saw a black bear in that area back before they were common to see in the state of Kentucky. We saw fox holes, deer, and rabbit, also. I still miss it there.

Life was wondrous for us back then. My life seems so boring now, with my 9:00 to 5:00 job. I miss being a little country girl!

1860 Lyra Nebula Vintage Image in Public Domain

Deer Scouting

By Jonathan Mullins

One Saturday in the fall 1994, my friend and I wanted go deer scouting. His papaw told us to get our stuff ready and he would take us.

We loaded up in his old grey Dodge truck and headed out the road. We were just happy to go to different part of the woods in our town. We pulled into the old hollow road where we were going.

My friend and I saw this big brown mountain lion with a tail about three-foot long. The cat was huge! It jumped from the road over a ditch line up onto the embankment. It was a jump of about six to eight feet on a steep hillside. It kept running up into the woods until we couldn't see it any more.

My friend said, "Papaw, did you see that?"

He said, "What was that?"

He had bad eye sight anyway but we said, "It was a cougar."

He replied, "Oh, you all must be seeing things. It kind of looked like a German shepherd to me."

We asked him, "Do you think German shepherds can leap six to eight feet from sitting still up on a bank?"

He got to thinking about it and turned around. We went to different place to scout!

Memorable Encounter
By Linda Berry

My story about the panther sighting happened at my home when I was a child. I was maybe fourth to fifth grade. We lived on property outside of Brevard, North Carolina, bordering the Pisgah National Forest.

My dad had slaughtered a pig one day and salted it down. It was lying on a table in our spare bedroom. Shortly after dark we heard a horrible noise. It sounded like scratching, crying, and screaming at our front door.

It brought us to our feet. We knew it was a mountain lion trying to break in. Dad grabbed the gun and ran toward the door. It fled but kept returning.

Another night we were awakened by our dogs raising sand. Mom got up and flipped the porch light on outside to see what was up. The light was blown. She walked outside anyway to check on the dogs.

Inside dad was still in bed trying to get mom back in the house. "Nannie Mae!" he yelled.

Outside mom said, "Ah, Lawrence! It's just a dog."

However, mom noticed it was behaving strangely. Every time she reached down to pet its head, it reached for her hand! And naturally mom didn't like it.

She scolded it. "You stop that," she said.

However, it kept swatting at her hand. As she smacked at it she noticed its ears. "That's odd," she said. "Its ears are short!"

Meanwhile back inside dad stumbled as he got out of bed and knocked something over. "Nannie Mae!" he said, "That might not be a dog! You better get back in here!"

Outside our visitor was spooked by dad's voice and became more agitated and aggressive toward mom. As dad headed through the living room it turned, ran across the porch and leaped over the highway in front of our house.

It was then we caught a glimpse of its sleek black body under the street light. Dads intuition was right. It wasn't a dog! It was a big black muscular cat!

It was a panther!

For as Long as I Can Remember!

By Veronica Brook Castle

I know for a fact that black panthers are still around here! At my grandmother's place where I grew up, there's been a black panther (or maybe more than one) for as long as I can remember.

The last time I saw one, it was about three years ago. I kept hearing something outside, so I turned on the porch light and looked out, I saw something huge dart down the yard and go across the road. I stepped out on the porch to see if I could get a closer look and saw it at the edge of our neighbor's fence (where they let their sheep and goats out to graze).

It was pacing back and forth like it was trying to figure out a way to get in. It was so massive every time its feet hit the ground, I heard it breathe and snarl. It was like nothing else I've ever seen before.

1830s – Robert Huish

"Here Kitty, Kitty"

By John Holbrook

I was working for Bledsoe Coal Company (in southeastern Kentucky) as an environmentalist collecting water samples in the silt ponds, water sheds, and from homes near the mines as was required for the NPDES permits. As I was driving on a rural dirt road in Leslie County, I saw what I thought was the most beautiful blue tinted black stray cat.

I stopped my truck and said to myself, "I'm going to take this cat home with me. I got out of the truck, got a sandwich out of my lunch box, and begin to walk towards the cat saying, "Here kitty, kitty," holding out the sandwich.

It didn't take too many steps and the cat stood up. The cat was about knee high in a crouch. It had a long tail that whipped around. It hissed at me!

I said to myself, "That ain't no regular stray cat!" and retreated back into the truck as fast as I could!

The next house I came to, I needed to get a water sample. I told them what I had just seen. The gentleman said, "Yes, I've seen it, too." Others had seen it in the area also.

Later that evening, I told one of my brother-in-laws about what happened. He didn't believe me.

About a month later, my brother-in-law and I were hunting in the deer woods. A big cat jumped up and ran near us. My brother-in-law said, "I believe you now because I just saw one with my own eyes!"

I've heard stories from others about people seeing big cats in Bell County, Kentucky.

I was out hunting late in the afternoon and I heard the scream of an animal that sounded like a woman screaming. Before I heard the scream, there were a lot of sounds in the forest. After the scream, all had turned very quiet! The hairs on the back of my neck stood straight up!

1830 Robert Huish – Public Domain

Panther Baby

By Sasha Connor

I remember when I was little we'd go to Jackson County, Kentucky and see my great uncle. He'd tell us about black panthers and stories.

My grandma has a story from when she was little. A baby panther came to their school house and they took it inside. The mother started circling the school house crying for her baby. The teacher had to slip the baby back out to get her to leave.

Big Tracks

By Gaddis Steven

I'm not sure if it was just an old mountain lion or a panther, but a few friends and I were sitting at a graveyard just above the house one night when the bear dogs started going crazy! We heard something run in the bushes. A few seconds later, we heard this terrifying scream that sounded like a woman screaming.

We loaded up and took off! We went back the next day and looked around. We found some pretty big tracks!

Big Cat in a Pine Tree
By Nick Armbrister

I live in the mountains of Virginia. When we were young, we could walk around at night camping and stuff. Our parents knew we were safe on our own. One time in the summer we were walking down this big hill and a panther was in a big pine tree. It started crying.

We looked up and saw it. We ran like crazy! When we got to the house, we stood on the porch and listened. It cried for hours, very close to the house. I can tell you that this experience was very scary!

For years we could hear it cry, but never saw that one again.

The second time I saw a panther, I was riding on a riding lawn mower, going to mow the grass in the church yard about two miles from my house. I rode by and saw it drinking water from a pond. This happened in the fall of the year about two years ago.

Ghost Panther
By Neal Powell

When I first moved to southern Rockcastle county just outside of Livingston, Kentucky in 1991, several of the old timers told me a story of a lady ghost walking throughout sandhill near Livingston with a black panther walking by her side.

A few years later after moving on Sandhill, I was driving down the backside of Sandhill that runs parallel to I-75 just around dusk. I saw a great big black panther standing right in the middle of the road! By the time I stopped my car I was only about thirty feet from the panther. It stared right at me and stood there for about three minutes.

Then just like that, it disappeared. I didn't see it walk away but just like that it was gone! I drove down that road every night for a year hoping to see that panther, but I never saw it again.

Yellow Panther

By Delia Frederick

I live in Highlands, North Carolina. I had a yellow panther in my yard. It happened early one morning as I was headed to work. When I saw it, we looked at each other standing still. Then we parted ways.

Panther in the Yard

By April Ashbrook

We have bobcats and black panthers here in eastern Kentucky around Natural Bridge. I had a black panther in my yard in February of 2003-4.

They were logging a farm in Rogers that butted next to mine. The black panther came through and out into my yard about 2:30 in the afternoon. I went out on the porch to see it.

Oh, my gosh! It surely reminds you where you belong on the food chain. I'm pretty sure it was an older one, it had gray on top of the black fur from the back of its head to the tip of its tail!

I lived on Glencarin Road when that happened.

Game Camera Photo

By Lara Eldridge

I have a photo taken by my game camera. It is on a trail that leads to Dube's Pond in Hooksett, New Hampshire. The picture was taken on August 5, 2016. We were in middle of historic drought and it was the first and only time we got the lion on camera.

My property abuts Bear Brook State Park, a 10,000 acre preserve. It is one of the largest parks in New Hampshire. We regularly see black bear, moose, bobcat, fisher cat, and fox. We also see huge coyotes that are a cross between eastern coyotes and Canadian timber wolves. They are quite large.

I have a close friend who works for the state. When I showed him the photo, he said, "Yes, he knows there are lions."

I asked why won't Fish and Game share that publicly? His reply was that if it was shared folks would come looking, hunting, and trapping trying to catch one of them. There are too few to have that happen and they need to be protected.

Like the Coyotes and Me

By Jerry Flanagan

I saw a brown mountain lion in the mid1960s. So, did my family. We were coming back from Moorefield, West Virginia, and were traveling towards Keyser, West Virginia on the Junction Road.

There are fields on the right side of the road. The mountain lion was sitting down at the edge where the creek is. My Dad pulled off the road and we got out of the car.

I ran toward it and got about fifty yards from it. It got up and started walking toward the creek. I could see its brown color clearly and the long tail. It looked like photos of the ones from out west. It was very big.

I think they stay around in these mountains just like the coyotes and me.

The Bobcat

By S. Hall

(Reprinted from a student project with Judith Victoria
Hensley at Wallins Elementary School and Junior High in Harlan
County, Kentucky)

One day my dad and I went deer hunting.
We were sitting and waiting for a deer to come
by. We heard something behind us and my dad
told me to be really quiet. I did what he said.

He said, "There is something in the
bushes."

We waited a few minutes and it came out.
It was a bobcat! We were really still and hoped
that it wouldn't know we were there. It just sat
there staring at us, like it wasn't sure what we
were.

I was scared, but after a few minutes it
went away. We went back to hunting. We were
walking through the woods and we came upon a
cave. Out came three bobcat kittens. We saw
the mother bobcat and understood why she had
been there staring at us.

After that we went the other way and were
looking for doe. We found a deer that was dead,
and something had been eating on it. My dad
knew it had been a bobcat that had done the
damage to the deer.

We went back home after that. I told my
mom and my brother about the bobcat and the

deer that we found that a bobcat had been eating on.

We saw the same bobcat and her kittens another day. The bobcat started killing our animals. My dad hid and watched overnight and saw the bobcat attacking our animals. He had no choice but to put a stop to it. It would have eaten the rest of our animals.

I asked my dad to wait another night before shooting the bobcat in case it went away. He agreed to wait one more night.

We watched, and it sat down in front of my sister's horse, named Dolly. When it heard the pigs oinking it went after them. My dad finally had no choice but to shoot it.

The kittens were still out there so my dad said we should try to take care of them. We tried to put food out for them, but it didn't last long. They ran away. We never saw them again after that. We kept looking out the windows hoping they might return and we'd at least know they were okay, but they never did.

Kramer Gary, U.S. Fish and Wildlife Service Public Domain Image

The Lynx
By D. Blanton

(Reprinted from a student project with Judith Victoria
Hensley at Wallins Elementary School and Junior High in Harlan
County, Kentucky)

My mom, my dad, uncle, cousin, my Nan
Napier, and I were in Middlesboro, Kentucky at
a pay lake. It was in the summer of 2007. We
would catch a lot of big fish over there. Mainly
we caught catfish.

We had only fished for about an hour
when my dad, cousin, and I went back to the
car. My dad had to walk us back there because
my cousin was scared of snakes. Mom and Nan
were hanging out in the car. Dad walked back
down to go fishing and left us at the car.

He was down there fishing for about an
hour when he spotted something black behind a
juice pole. He couldn't tell for sure what it was
at first, so he kept watching it. He saw its tail
start wagging and it stuck its head out a little
from behind the juice pole where he could see it.

It was acting like it was hiding from my
dad and thought he couldn't see it, as if maybe
it was planning on attacking my dad or
something. My dad picked up a rock and threw
at it. It came out from behind the juice pole he
saw the whole cat. It was a huge lynx. It was

nothing but muscle, with no fat on it. It took off up in the mountains.

My uncle had been to the store buying a fishing pole and he did not see it. When dad told him about the big cat, he decided to stay at the car with the rest of us.

Dad kept fishing in that same spot and about an hour later the lynx started walking right back down the mountain side toward him. Dad picked up another rock and threw at it again. It ran and hid behind the same juice pole where it was at first. He figured it would go away again, but it started inching its way over toward him, a little bit at a time.

He decided to get the fishing poles and stuff and come back up to the car. He sat in the car with the rest of us and we all watched that big lynx from inside the vehicle.

It went over to where he had been sitting with his fishing pole and was sniffing around.

A few days later my dad talked to some other guys who were fishing there. He asked them if they had seen anything strange around there. They told him they had seen a big black cat walking around. They said it looked like a lynx to them, too.

We went back to that same spot last week-end. We heard a lot of stuff up in the woods. We heard twigs snapping and leaves crunching. My dad wondered if it was that same lynx again roaming around. Maybe it was, or maybe it had babies that had grown up in the last four years that were hanging around that same area.

He decided he wants to take us back there this week-end and go fishing. It is a really good fishing spot. He catches a lot of fish in that one place. They will even come up and splash the water.

He said he is going to take a camera with us this time. My uncle has a motion camera. Maybe he will let us set it up around that same spot and see what is roaming around over there in the woods.

Another day my uncle and I were bow hunting in deer season. We were up in the mountains and had set there all morning, freezing. We took a snack break and went on down the mountain. We thought we heard a deer once, and then a little later heard the noise again.

It was three bobcats! They were all grown. It was legal to shoot one with a bow. We followed their tracks and came upon one of them separated from the others. My uncle shot it with the bow and had it stuffed and mounted. It is still at this house.

The Bobcat in the Coal Mine

By D. Blanton

(Reprinted from a student project with Judith Victoria
Hensley at Wallins Elementary School and Junior High in Harlan
County, Kentucky)

Yesterday when my dad came home from work he told me an interesting bobcat story. He works for a coal mine called Manalapan located at Happy Top, Kentucky. There is also another coal mine down below where he works called Mine #8.

As soon as the men came in to work yesterday, their boss told them to watch out.

My dad asked, "Why?"

The Boss said, "There was a report that someone had seen a bobcat inside the mine."

The mine where my dad works is called "low coal." The space is so small, it's only about 36 inches of room to work, but that is just the right height for a bobcat to walk in.

The "Miner" machine is really huge and loud. There are loggers working over top of the mine, also. Sometimes when a big tree comes down, they can hear it inside the mine. It will "pop" the top of the mine. My dad is a roof bolter.

Inside the coal mine is a noisy place. When the machinery started up, my dad saw the bobcat go running out of the mine. I don't

think the bobcat was expecting all that noise
when he went snooping around inside the mine!

*Wikimedia Commons – Photo from an employee of the United States
Department of Fish and Wildlife Service*

A Bobcat in Smith, Kentucky

By Chelsey Caldwell as told by Eugene Asher

(Reprinted from a student project with Judith Victoria Hensley at Wallins Elementary School and Junior High in Harlan County, Kentucky)

On Friday, November 11, 2011, the day before rifle season, I went deer scouting up in Smith, Kentucky. I was about two and a half hours up the mountain.

I got out of my silver Dodge truck and looked around. It looked like a good place for deer.

Suddenly, I lost my balance in a slick spot. I fell, hitting my back and shoulders and slid down the mountain upside down! I was grabbing at sticks and rocks, trying to stop myself.

Finally, I caught hold of some sticky briars, which was very painful, but I was glad that I had a grasp on something that had stopped my slide down the mountain. After I was sure that I was completely stopped and safe to let go, I released the briar and had to climb all the way back up the mountain to my truck. I sure was glad to get inside my vehicle!

I headed off the mountain and had been driving for about an hour and a half after my accident. The sun was setting. I was driving slow and still looking for deer sign along the way. Unexpectedly I saw a bobcat. I stared at him and he stared at me.

I was thinking about shooting it with my .17 caliber, and then it hit me that it wasn't bobcat season. I would not shoot it out of season.

After staring at me briefly, the bobcat ran down the right side of the road and jumped up the left side of the road and ran into the weeds. His coloring quickly made him invisible in the weeds. I stared after him a little while, but he was long gone.

I ran on home, to rest up for deer hunting. I still have scrapes and bruises from my fall, but I was lucky that I wasn't hurt worse than that!

Image from Wikimedia Commons Public Domain – Photo by Calbookaddict 2006 in Almaden Quicksilver County Park

My Dad's Adventure with a Wildcat

By L. Felker

(Reprinted from a student project with Judith Victoria Hensley at Wallins Elementary School, Harlan County, Kentucky)

It was a cold dark night back in 2003. My family and I were moving from Wallins Creek, Kentucky to Dryden, Virginia. My father went to get the last load of our belongings, which included his tools, out of the old dairy that was located out behind the house.

He stepped into the dairy and a solid black wildcat of some sort attacked him! He had to protect his head and neck so it wouldn't kill him. All he could reach to defend himself was a steel pipe. He grabbed the pipe and swung at the cat as much as he could. He must have got in a few good licks because finally the wildcat stopped attacking and walked away.

My dad had to go to the Emergency Room for treatment. He was lucky that he didn't have any broken bones and none of the scratches were deep enough to require stitches.

The wildcat had bitten his hand and scratched up his arm. He had to have twenty rabies shots since there was no wildcat body to examine and make sure it wasn't carrying rabies. The wildcat's behavior was so abnormal, they had to give my dad the shots just in case the wildcat did have rabies. That was the only way to be sure he would be okay.

In the Right Place at the Right Time

By Judith Victoria Hensley

In the days before I knew where to find the newly released elk in the mountains of Southeastern Kentucky, I made a lot of unsuccessful attempts to find them. I even paid to go on elk tours, but the elk we saw were always at a great distance.

I had heard that there was a herd of elk over on Jewel Ridge. I drove through the Cumberland end of Kingdom Come State park, out Little Shepherd Trail toward Leatherwood and the Lily Cornett Woods. Finally, a friend and I found an old abandoned mining road at the base of Jewel Ridge. We had heard that the elk grazed in those fields back on the mountain.

We had turned up the gravely dirt road and driven maybe a quarter or half of a mile when something jumped out in the road in front of us.

We had been looking for elk and certainly not expecting to see anything else. Because I had hoped to see an elk, I had my camera already in my hand and turned on. But I was so shocked I sat there for a while before I did anything.

"Oh, my gosh!" I screamed.

Photos by Judith V. Hensley – Jewel Ridge, KY

I remembered the camera in my hand and tried to zoom in on the big cat through the windshield. I started clicking.

Out of the tall weeds popped one little bobcat, followed by a second little bobcat, and finally a third little one emerged. I kept clicking, but they were spread out and I didn't get them all in the same photo. The first big cat was about the size of a German shepherd and the little ones were about the size of beagles.

I had stopped the car and was still trying to get photos through the front windshield with my zoom lens. I was so excited it's a miracle that any of the photos turned out. Only a few did, but the results are in the following two photos.

What I thought at first might be a cougar, once the photos were developed, turned out definitely to be a big bobcat or lynx and her

three cubs. The main differences that proved
she wasn't a mountain lion was her short tail
and her whiskers. This was a once in a lifetime
opportunity and I am very thankful that I got
these shots before all four cats crossed the road
into the tall weeds and vanished from sight.

Photos by Judith Victoria Hensley – Jewell Ridge, KY

Enos and the Wildcat

By Ernest Hensley

When we were kids, one of our favorite things to do when we weren't working around the land was for us boys to hunt. We had fourteen children in our family and all of my brothers, Dad, and I were hunters. Dad always kept a pack of the best hunting dogs to be found anywhere in Harlan County.

My favorite dog out of the pack was Watch. If he got on the trail of an animal, that animal might as well know that his time had come.

All of us boys knew how to hunt, fish, and trap. I had set a trap and my little brother, Enos, went with me to check it out. Sure enough, there was a wild cat in it. It was the prettiest cat I had ever laid my eyes on! I didn't want to skin it. I wanted to keep it! While I was trying to get it out of the trap, it managed to get away.

It wasn't long before we heard Watch set up a howl on the Upland Ridge and we knew he had something treed. We went to him to see what animal was dumb enough to cross old Watch. I looked up in the tree and there sat the wild cat. It was one of the biggest wild cats I had ever seen in my life. It wasn't a mountain wildcat, a bobcat, but a house cat that had lived in the mountains and was wild (a feral cat).

I climbed the tree and the cat was more scared of the dog than he was of me. He wouldn't jump out where the dog could get him, so when I got within reach of the cat, I stretched my arm and hand out to take hold of him and he stretched out to take hold of me! He got me right in the hand with his teeth and hung on. I shoved his two front feet together, grabbed both hind feet together and stuck him under my arm. That was no easy trick.

I held on to him for dear life coming down out of that tree because I knew if I let go, I had had it. My brother, Enos, was standing at the foot of the tree and I made him take the cat when I got down far enough to hand it over to him. The cat started clawing and biting at him. He started hollering, "I can't hold him! He's tearing me up!"

I hollered back at Enos, "YOU BETTER HOLD HIM!" Well, he was more scared of me than he was of the wild cat, so he held him until I got out of the tree and took him back.

I took him home and put him in the house. He was such a pretty cat, I thought to myself, "We'll keep this cat!" We were both just kids and we didn't realize how much trouble a feral cat could be if you tried to close it up inside a house.

I closed up all the windows and doors so he couldn't escape. I only remember Enos and I being the only ones in the house when all of this went on.

It didn't take long to figure out there would be no keeping that cat! He truly was a wild cat. He would run and jump at the windows, trying to get the windows out and then I would be in BIG trouble if he broke one.

It didn't take long for me to realize what a bad idea I had had in trying to bring that cat home and make a housecat out of him! When I opened the door, two of our big dogs were standing outside the door waiting for him. That cat whipped both of those dogs and left that place in a streak! Enos and I were both glad to see him go!

Public Domain Image – Wikimedia Commons – David R. Tribble, Bobcat Kittens in North Texas June 29, 2012

Bobcat Road Kill

By Ben Begley

(Former Director of Environmental Education at Pine
Mountain Settlement School in Harlan County, Kentucky, and
recently retired)

I have been a biologist for twenty-five years
and started studying biology about thirty years
ago. I have seen bobcats in the wild only about
ten times in all of those years.

I saw one that had been hit by a vehicle
early one morning. It had been run over and
was lying beside of the road. It had happened
some time in the night.

I have a permit to pick up road kills and
remount them and things like that. When I
drove by, I realized it was a bobcat. I went on
up and turned around. I didn't go more than
half of a mile before I found a place to turn
around and go back.

I intended to go back, pick it up, and
mount it as a specimen. It was really a good
one. It didn't have any disfiguration. It hadn't
been mangled by the car that hit it.

By the time I got back to the spot,
someone else had already picked it up and was
gone. That's a good example of how valued their
pelts are. I really wish I could have gotten that
bobcat. He would have made a beautiful

specimen to show students when they come to Pine Mountain Settlement School.

There are questions about whether or not bobcats are being released into this area. To my knowledge, this hasn't taken place.

The populations of a specific animal within a given territory will rise and fall depending on food. Bobcats mostly feed on smaller rodents, and rabbits. If there is a good rabbit population the chances are that there will be a good bobcat population and a good coyote population.

There is a good supply of food for bobcats in Kentucky. Therefore, the bobcat population is usually pretty healthy. The reason people don't see them more often is because they are elusive animals which hunt at night. Their food source is in the wild and they really have no reason to be hanging around in human territory.

Photo by Judith Victoria Hensley
Begley Wildlife Management Area Pine Mountain, KY

Panther on the Road

By L. Brock

(Reprinted from a student project with Judith Victoria Hensley at Wallins Elementary School and Junior High in Harlan County, Kentucky)

My husband and I were driving back from Harlan one evening in the summer of 2011. We were on Highway 119 between Coldiron and Molus, Kentucky.

He saw something black beside of the road and said, "What is that?"

I looked and saw what he was talking about.

He said, "Is that a panther?"

I said, "Well, it looks like some kind of cat."

It ran across the road in front of our car about twenty yards away and we both saw it clearly. It was jet black and as big as a large sized dog. The thing that stood out in my mind was the long black tail behind it. It was fat and perfectly round following out behind the animal.

It moved like a big cat, kind of like pouncing as it leapt across the road and went up into the mountains. It ran on the road, but it leapt as it went up into the mountains.

We thought for sure that it was a panther, but we neither one wanted to say anything because neither of us had ever seen one before and had never heard of one being around here before. We kept it to ourselves because we just didn't want people thinking we were crazy for saying we had seen a panther crossing a main road.

We were studying about animals this year in Mrs. Donna Hensley's class and she was telling the students about a panther being back up in the mountains behind her house.

I went home and told my husband that we were not the only ones who had seen a panther in the area. I've also heard about one man who has seen them in his barn up above our house.

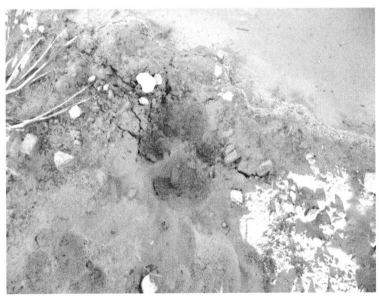

Photo by Judith Victoria Hensley – Pine Mountain, KY

No One Believed It

By Chelsey Caldwell

(As told by Allyson Asher Caldwell)

(Reprinted from a student project with Judith Victoria Hensley at Wallins Elementary School and Junior High in Harlan County, Kentucky)

On the last day of deer rifle season 2010, my husband, George, asked Faith and me to look for deer with him on the strip job where he worked in Coldiron, Kentucky. It had snowed that morning or the night before and a light skiff of snow was still lying on the ground. The sun was shining bright and the sky was clear blue.

We drove around for hours and didn't see a single deer! Then we went to another spot to look. That road was covered in ice and we had to turn around and go back. It was too dangerous to try to go on.

I was looking out the window on the passenger's side as I turned and I could see the steep embankment of the mountain. I got a glimpse of something moving on a bend in the hillside. At first, it looked like a fleeting shadow – until I realized that it had ears!

I thought it was a bear at first. I kept watching it, trying to get a better look. It moved a certain way and I recognized the cat's head and long swooping tail.

"Oh, my gosh!" I shouted. "It's a black panther!" I couldn't wait to tell my husband.

We were already almost even with the panther and the hill was straight up. We were too close to see the whole hillside or where the panther went.

A security guard came over to us who didn't recognize us or that George worked on that site for the company. He drew my attention and I lost sight of the spot where the panther was going up the mountain.

There was a big boulder with an overhang and I think it went under there. I didn't see it again and no one else with me saw it at all.

There were some men who worked on that mining site who said they had also seen it. It had been roaming around in that area.

No one believes that I actually saw a black panther that day in Forester's Creek, but I know what I saw, and it was real.

Public Domain Image - 1914

Big Cats in Harlan County, Kentucky
By Mark Taylor
(Reprinted from a student project with Judith Victoria
Hensley at Wallins Elementary School and Junior High in Harlan
County, Kentucky)

My only real sighting of a mountain lion, or panther, occurred at Black Star one spring about nine years ago, while turkey hunting alone. I heard a turkey gobbling off in the distance, and I was sneaking around an old coal level trying to cut down the distance between us.

I kept easing on around, quietly, using my caller, so he would think I was coming closer to him. I heard leaves rustling up above me and thought I must have somehow gotten around in front of him.

Unexpectedly, a big black cat shot across the road and down the hill directly in front of me. Although he was moving fast, I got a good look at him. He was solid muscle from nose to tail tip. The afternoon sun glinted off his deep black fur, and a thick tail nearly as long as his body trailed out behind him.

I judged him to weigh 50 or 60 lbs. I ran over to the edge of the road and looked over, trying to see which way he went. Although there was 100 yards of open space, he was nowhere to be found.

I've never seen anything move that fast. He was gone!

I killed my big gobbler, though, and as it was the last day of the season, I was mighty glad.

Though I've never seen another mountain lion, I've seen their tracks on Daniels Mountain and on Pine Mountain and have felt my hair stand on end a few times, certain I was being tracked by the silent, but sure footed big cats.

Photo submitted by Laura Johnson Curry – Baxter, Kentucky

The Panther that Ruined our Deer Hunt

(Reprinted from a student project with Judith Victoria Hensley at Wallins Elementary School and Junior High in Harlan County, Kentucky)

By J. Saylor

I was so excited about going deer hunting with my dad the next morning that I was ready to dive in the bed and go straight to sleep. My mom got a whiff of me and she made me go take a shower.

I hurried in and out of the shower and toweled off. I wiped the condensation off of the window and hopped in bed.

We set the alarm clock for 6:00 a.m.

I rolled out as soon as the alarm went off and woke my dad. We got ready in a hurry and I told him to go get the guns and shells. We told mom where we would be hunting and dived out the back door.

We drove to an old rocky hill and got out of the truck. We climbed to the top, lay down, and loaded our guns. We put them about one foot away from us after they were loaded.

I said, "Safety first!"

About forty-five minutes later, a six point and an eight-point buck came into view. I took aim on the eight-point, but when I was going to fire, a cougar came out of nowhere. It took its humongous paws and hit the deer in the back. The six-pointer ran back off into the woods.

The cougar's muscles tightened up and every move it made, its muscles showed. Every time the deer moved, the cougar tightened up on it. Then it jumped on the deer's back, then latched its jaws around the deer's neck and took it down. It killed the deer while we watched.

That cougar was about thirty feet away from me and I got my camera out. Before I could get it turned on, the cougar was gone in just a second. It dragged the deer off with it, dripping in blood.

We did not dare to get up for a while. When we did, there was no sign of my deer.

Edward Lloyd - 1896

Panther in the Dog House

(Reprinted from a student project with Judith Victoria
Hensley at Wallins Elementary School and Junior High in Harlan
County, Kentucky)

By Franklin Smith

It was in that part of November when the
nights are cold and chill, and the frosts have set
in. I remember that my dad had passed away a
year or two earlier, so it was between 1987 and
1989.

My family and I were in the family room
watching television around 8:00 p.m.   I had
been eating a snack. When I was done I got up
to carry my plate back to the kitchen and put
my dish in the sink.

As I was standing at the sink I looked out
the window and across the yard at the dog
house. There was Rover, standing outside the
doghouse with his head stuck inside eating.
That was a little peculiar. Rover had been dad's
big black dog that he loved very much. We all
loved that dog because dad had loved him so
much.

I put my dish in the sink and started
walking toward my bedroom when it hit me that
Rover wasn't that big. Whatever was out there
was so big it would have had trouble getting in
Rover's doghouse. Maybe it was a stray helping
himself to Rover's food.

I went into the dining room where the view was clearer and on the ground level, even with the doghouse. I looked out the dining room sliding door and saw it plain as day - a big black panther! I could tell by the long, round tail, and the huge muscles in its haunches.

I grabbed the 30/30, cocked it and slowly tried to open the sliding door without making any noise. But as soon as I did, the panther pulled its head out of the doghouse.

That big black head was huge! It turned, took one look at me with its golden eyes, and it was gone. I didn't even have time to raise the gun up.

Vintage Public Domain Image - drawing by James Hope
Stewart published in 1843 in "The Naturalist's Library, Mammalia, Vol. 1,
Cats"

The Mountain Lion

By D. Blanton

(Reprinted from a student project with Judith Victoria
Hensley at Wallins Elementary School and Junior High in Harlan
County, Kentucky)

I was at my house one day and my dog
started barking a lot. It started at night time,
but I was still outside riding my dirt bike
around the neighborhood. I decided to ride my
dirt bike over there to see what my dog was a
barking at. I went over to her and I heard these
weird noises in the woods like twigs snapping
and big crack sounds

I thought it was a deer, maybe. I walked
into a field close by to get a better look. I wasn't
afraid of a deer, but when I got over there it
turned out not to be a deer. As I was walking in
the field I saw big fresh cat prints! I felt really
weird because I thought it was there watching
me.

There is a river that runs past that field
and I looked over there and saw a BIG
mountain lion. I stood there and watched it.
Then I started walking backwards slowly until I
couldn't see it any more. When I got out of
sight, I turned around and ran back home and
got my dad.

He hurried and grabbed his mining light
and took off in the direction I told him. I was

running to keep up with him, but he was just walking really fast.

When we got there, he shined his light over across the river and the mountain lion was walking in shallow water. We watched it for about an hour and then it just went back up in the mountains.

It was a big yellow mountain lion with a lot of muscle!

Free Usage from 4FreePhotos.com

Panther in the Snow

(Reprinted from a student project with Judith Victoria
Hensley at Wallins Elementary School and Junior High in Harlan
County, Kentucky)

By Dusty Alred

When I was a young man living in Loyall, Kentucky, I saw the only black panther I've ever seen. It had been snowing and the road was covered white and icy.

I was going to my friend, Creed Turner's, house who lived in Keith, Kentucky. I was driving carefully on Conley Loop off of Highway 119, and going pretty slow on the snow. Up ahead I caught a glimpse of something running on the road going the same direction as my car. I could make out that it was a black cat.

As I got a little closer I thought, *"That is a BIG house cat!"*

I was driving about twenty miles per hour because the roads were so slick but was still gaining a little on the cat. As I got closer to it, I realized it was no house cat! I could see its hunches and muscles in the back and that long black tail flowing out behind it. I could see the muscles working in its shoulders as it ran. It was staying right in front of me on the road, running about the speed I was driving.

Finally, it cut across the road in front of me and took off up into the woods. By that time, I was very close to it and there was no mistaking what I had seen. I've heard people tell about seeing black panthers through the years, but that was it for me to actually see in person.

It makes sense, though, that panthers would be here in the forests where there are plenty of deer and game to eat. Back behind Keith (the place where my friend lived) is Blanton Forest, which covers thousands of acres. It is a wilderness area where any kind of wild animal could live and thrive.

We used to go hiking through the forest all the time when we were young, back in behind the Boy Scout Camp. I've seen a lot of things, and heard things, but that was the only time I ever got to see a black panther.

Vintage Public Domain Image of Peter Quivey and the Mountain Lion, oil on canvas painting by Charles Christian Nahl, 1858

The Long Black Tail

(Reprinted from a student project with Judith Victoria Hensley at Wallins Elementary School and Junior High in Harlan County, Kentucky)

By Sasha Patterson

(As told by Juanita Lee)

Water Tank Road in Wallins Creek, Kentucky sits off to itself between the river, railroad track, and the foot of the mountain. That's where I live with my Mamaw, Juanita Lee. Our house is a two-story brown house and it has a porch on the front and the back. We sit out there in the evenings, usually after all the work is done.

About three years ago in late spring, Mamaw was sitting out on the front porch. You can see down the road and the mountain at the same time when you sit on that porch.

She heard the dogs start barking and she looked down the road to see what all that barking was about. At first, she saw something black and thought it was just a big old black house cat. She watched it and realized that it was too far away and too big to be a house cat.

One of our neighbors has a goat field and that's w here the big black cat appeared. When she saw it closer, she realized it was as big as a hunting dog!

It jumped across the road and went up into the woods. It is a one lane road big enough for one car to travel on at a time. The big cat jumped clear across that road in one leap. Then she saw its long black tail behind it.

She said that cat was pitch black and its tail was long and round, about as long as the cat's body – just a little bit shorter.

She was sure she had seen a panther. We have always known that we have panthers around there. Other people have seen them, and other people have seen their tracks by the river. Sometimes in the middle of the night, the dogs start barking and having a fit, but we don't know for sure what is out there. It could be because of the panther that Mamaw saw.

Robert Huish 1830

Trash Puppy

(Reprinted from a student project with Judith Victoria
Hensley at Wallins Elementary School and Junior High in Harlan
County, Kentucky)

By J. Thomas

One fine morning, my dog, Trash Puppy, and I were on our morning walk. Trash Puppy was silver and black in color with two white spots on the top of his forehead. He had two shiny blue eyes. Everyone loved Trash Puppy, and I did, too!

We were going on our morning walk. Trash Puppy and I went everywhere together. Even when I went to school, he would wait until I got off the bus and he would walk me home.

One week-end Trash Puppy had to be tied up outside. When my dad was asleep, I went outside to play in the back yard. While I was playing, I saw something big and black. It was a big black cat and it had a long black tail. Its eyes were big and yellowish-gold. I knew it was a panther. I had seen pictures of them, but I never ever expected to see one in person!

Trash Puppy started to bark. The panther started to come toward me. I ran toward the house, but my foot got hung in a hole while I was running. Just when the panther was about to pounce on me, Trash Puppy jumped in front of me and was barking his head off.

Trash puppy jumped on the panther and tried to bite it on the neck to scare it away. The panther took its big paw and knocked Trash Puppy off. The panther's claws had ripped open Trash Puppy's side. The panther ran away.

Trash Puppy was really hurt, but he still came over and got in my lap and licked my face. He was worried about me instead of about the big gash in his side.

I went inside to get my dad. He came out and looked at Trash Puppy. Trash Puppy was losing a lot of blood. We wrapped his side and wrapped him in a shirt and took him to his dog house.

That night I couldn't sleep, so I went outside to check on Trash Puppy. When I got in there, in his dog house with him, he wasn't breathing. I fell to my knees and started to cry. I never left his side that night, but when I fell asleep, my dad carried me inside.

The next morning, I went to check on him and he was gone. I never saw him again.

Cat tracks on Pine Mountain on the Harlan County/Bell County Line, Kentucky Photo by Judith V. Hensley – Size 8 adult foot.

Panther on the Mountain

By Rachel Johnson

One warm summer evening one of my cousins and I were riding across the mountain at the Begley Wildlife Management Area which sits on the Harlan County/Bell County Line on Pine Mountain. We went looking for wildlife occasionally in different places. We had gone several times to Kingdom Come State Park in Cumberland, Kentucky, looking for bear and had seen them several times.

This day, we were looking for elk, or wild horses, and had heard a rumor about a panther reported to have recently been seen in that area. We just hoped to see any kind of wildlife and my cousin hoped to maybe get a few good photos. We had driven around for about an hour, hoping we may see some elk or other wild animals out for their evening snack.

My cousin was driving up the mountain and at the same time, we both spotted something standing on the ridge in front of us. It was very large, and black with a long tail. It looked like a big black panther straight out of *Jungle Book*.

We stopped the car and we both watched it without saying a word. After it disappeared, she asked me what I had seen. I told her I wasn't positive, but I sure thought it had been a panther. She thought the same thing. I had never seen anything else like it in my entire life – as black as night, with muscles rippling in the sun and a long black cylindrical tail stretching out behind it. There was nothing between us and the big cat, and no mistaking what we had seen.

It was crouched down at the top of the ridge as if it was stalking something, moving slowly and deliberately close to the ground. Its muscles rippled with every move. Whatever it was after probably didn't stand a chance. It went over the top of the ridge and out of sight.

We did not get any photos. It was such a shock and happened so quickly, we both had cameras and neither one of us even thought about trying to get a picture.

We have been back there several times, and still haven't seen the panther again. We have seen some very large cat tracks in the mud. I would love to see the panther again, but only from the safety of the car.

Public Domain Image from Wikimedia Commons CCO

The Mountain Lion and the Deer Hunt

(Reprinted from a student project with Judith Victoria Hensley at Wallins Elementary School and Junior High in Harlan County, Kentucky)

By K. Sumpter

One day my dad went deer hunting. While he was in the woods just waiting for a deer to come, he thought he heard something near him. He looked around and he didn't see anything. He eased himself over to where he thought he heard the noise. When he went over there, he didn't see a thing.

He walked back over to a tree and waited, and then waited some more. Deer hunters have to be patient. Some-times they sit in the same spot for hours waiting for a deer to come along.

Then all of a sudden, he heard that noise again. When he turned around, he saw a big mountain lion!

He fired his gun up in the air to scare the mountain lion away. Sure enough, at the sound of his gun, the mountain lion turned and ran off back into the wild.

Stalked by a Panther

By D. Gailey, as told by Karen Lindsey

(Reprinted from a student project with Judith Victoria
Hensley at Wallins Elementary School and Junior High in Harlan
County, Kentucky)

Long ago not all people in our part of the
state could afford cars. As a result of that, if you
wanted to go to town, church, or school, you
had to walk. People walked almost everywhere
they went.

My grandmother, Lee Hensley, and my
aunt, Eleanor Bouley, were walking home from
a church service they had just attended at
Ephraim Osborne's church in Wallins,
Kentucky. That meant they had walked there
before service and had to walk back home, even
though it was after dark.

The route they walked home was up Happy
Top. Happy Top is a little community at the top
of the mountain with no street lights at all.
When night falls, it is a very dark place
surrounded by mountains on both sides of the
road.

When they started out on their journey,
they were walking with Maggie Moore and Mrs.
Hopkins. Everything went fine until they parted
ways at Maggie's house and started up the
steepest part of the mountain. As Mamaw,
Eleanor, and Mrs. Hopkins walked, they began

to hear some form of animal walking in the woods to the left of the road.

At first, they thought it was a deer. The woods were full of deer. Soon they began to notice that when they would stop to listen, the animal would stop, too. The group realized that no deer would follow them, and this really frightened them!

When they reached Mrs. Hopkins house, she begged them to stay with her. My family has always trusted in God and Mamaw quickly told Mrs. Hopkins not to worry because the Lord would watch over them.

As they neared the side road on which we live (Ringeye Lane), they began to quicken their pace. When they did, so did the animal. Mamaw told me herself that it felt like her heart was going to beat right out of her chest from fear!

Within twenty feet of their front porch, the animal let out a scream that sounded just like a woman's scream. When they looked behind them, they saw a black animal with a long tail come out of the brush. Needless to say, they broke into a run for their lives.

Papaw was sitting in the living room when Mamaw and Eleanor came running in the house. I have often heard him say, "I thought they had torn the door clean off the hinges."

He got his shotgun and went outside to see if he could kill it, but as usual, it was gone.

The panther is a very elusive creature which some people in our state claim do not exist in Kentucky. All I know is that seeing is believing! Once you have come face to face with one, especially in the dark of night, you will believe and no one on earth could make you doubt what you have seen!

Public Domain Image - painted for Outing magazine by Carl Runguis 1899

Edward Lloyd – 1898

Early Morning Visitor

(Reprinted from a student project with Judith Victoria
Hensley at Wallins Elementary School and Junior High in Harlan
County, Kentucky)

By K. Sumpter

My mom has a habit of drinking her coffee
every morning before she does anything else.
One morning she made her coffee, poured some
in her little coffee cup, and enjoyed it very
much.

When she was finished, she sat her cup
down and opened the back door to look out over
the yard. She saw something unusual lying in
the back yard; something black. She stepped
out onto the porch in order to get a better look
at the black thing.

It stood up and she realized it was a black
panther!

She ran back inside to get my dad's
hunting gun. She stepped back out on the
porch and the big black cat was still there. She
fired into the air once, thinking the noise would
scare the panther away. It didn't. Instead of
running, it came closer to the porch!

She fired a second time into the air. It just
looked up at her as if it was no big deal, but
then turned and ran away, back into the woods,
back with its own kind.

Monkey's Eyebrow
By Judith Victoria Hensley

I grew up in the city, right outside of
Chicago. But I never got the mountains out of
my blood or out of my soul. When I was old
enough to go to college, I chose to come back to
the region and attended the University of the
Cumberlands (then known as Cumberland
College).

Sarah Boggs (now married to Bill Conatser)
became one of my best friends. She was from
McCreary County, Kentucky and her family
invited me home with her many, many times. I
loved going home with her and spending time
with her family and having excursions in the
mountains.

Sarah's dad, Elmer Boggs, was the County
Extension Agent whose position was through
the University of Kentucky. Her mother, Irene,
was actively involved in church and community.

Even after I was married, my former
husband, and I continued to spend time with
Sarah's parents. They were wonderful,
welcoming people who always made others feel
at home.

I had told Don tales about panther in
Harlan County that I had heard growing up and
their screams that I had heard for myself as

they echoed off the ridges in the dark at my
Grandfather, Enos Hensley's, house in Martin's
Fork (also known as Smith), Kentucky. He
didn't believe me.

There were tales In McCreary County
about panther, also. He didn't believe those
either.

One week-end Sarah's parents, Don, and I
had all been up to their cabin on Parker's
Mountain. On Sunday, we packed up and
headed back off the mountain. When we got to
the foot of the mountain at the Post Office at
Monkey's Eyebrow, Irene Boggs realized she had
left her glasses at the cabin. Elmer turned the
truck around and we headed back up to retrieve
the forgotten glasses.

A huge panther leapt across the road right
in front of the truck, there at Monkey's
Eyebrow. It had only been ten or twenty feet in
front of us. There was no mistaking what we'd
seen.

I looked at Don's face and he looked like
he'd seen a ghost. He never doubted any tale he
heard after that about panthers. His brother,
Alan, was a different story.

The Boggs family was generous with their
cabin. They let us go camping in the Parker's
Mountain cabin one week-end on our own. We
took Alan with us.

Hearing the story of the panther, Alan
wanted to see one. and I hoped to photograph

one. We came up with a really dumb idea. We would bait the ditch across the road from the cabin, thinking that if any animals showed up, we could see them, or I could photograph them.

We left some hamburger meat or something over there, and sort of forgot about it while we had dinner. After we had eaten, I decided to rake all our scraps and leftovers together and carry them out to that same spot.

The only trouble was that it was after dark. There I went with a skillet full of scraps into the darkness. I sensed something there and turned back and ran toward the cabin. I heard whatever it was running behind me. I barely made it in the screen door and slammed the wooden door behind me, scared to death. I heard something jump up on the porch.

Don and Alan were making fun of me for being a scaredy cat. Alan said, "I'll go out there and if anything is really out there, I'll hit it in the head with this rock and shoot it with this pistol."

He picked up a big rock in his left hand that he had found and thought it might be a fossil or an Indian artifact. He drew out his pistol in his right hand and out the door he went into the black night.

About five or ten seconds later, he came flying back in the door and slammed it behind

him. "There's really something out there!" he
exclaimed.

His eyes were as big as saucers. He still
had the rock in one hand and the unfired pistol
in the other.

We listened and could hear something big
pacing back and forth on the front porch.
Occasionally, it sounded like it was rubbing up
against the screen door. They were both so
scared, they wouldn't even go back out to the
bathroom all night.

We built up the fire and stayed quietly
there listening to the stillness of the night and
all of the eerie woodland sounds, wondering
what was out there, just on the other side of the
door. I'm not sure how much sleep any of us got
that night. We were all ready to pack up our
gear and head back down the mountain the
next morning. Alan never went back to the
cabin again with us after that.

I guess I wasn't the only scaredy cat in the
bunch!

Vintage Public domain image

How to Handle a Painter (Panther)

As Told by the Late Harvey Wilson of Martin's Fork, KY

(Reprinted from a student project *from Harlan County and Its People* with Judith Victoria Hensley at Wallins Elementary School and Junior High in Harlan County, Kentucky)

My granddaddy Lee was coming back across the Brush Mountain from having been over in Virginia and it was getting along about dark. There were always tales of people seeing or being chased by painters (panthers), so he was a little nervous about coming across that wilderness nigh on to dark. Painters prowl in search of game in the dark.

Granddaddy had heard that if you take your hat off, and stick it over your face, run at the painter, and bark like a dog, they would run off. He was thinking about that when he came up to the top of the mountain by the rock they call Painter Rock.

Sure enough, right there, lying right on top of that rock waiting for someone to come along was this big old painter. Granddaddy had to cross through that Gap to get on home and he didn't stand a chance of outrunning that big cat if it got after him.

He took off his hat, put it over his face, and started barking like a dog, just like he had

heard to do if you met up with a painter. Well,
that big old black painter took off running right
down through the mountain, there.
Granddaddy Lee took off running and came on
home.

A little while after that, up here where
John Howard used to live, the road used to run
down the other side of the creek instead of
running down this side where it is now.
Granddaddy Lee started to cross the creek and
there laid a big painter on a rock. Right by the
road, it was. He cracked down on that painter
with a rock and hit it right between the eyes!
He said it turned a somersault to get going away
from him!

Grandma Wilson use to tell some big
stories about bears and things. Her name was
Mary Anna Wilson

Grandma would tell about a painter or a
bear that ate people or run them (chased them).
Grandma said that one time a painter got after
one woman on horseback who was packing her
baby with her in the saddle. She had to throw
her baby off the horse to keep it from getting
both of them.

Painters were common in these mountains
back in those days. People might not see them
as often as they use to, but they are still here,
right up in these mountains. There are still
plenty signs of them.

The Birthing

By Charleen Rose

There is a family story about a panther
and the night my great-great-grandfather was
born. The story goes like this:

The night my great-great-grandfather was
being born, a black painter climbed on the roof
of the old log house. They believed it was
sensing that a child was being born.

With my great-great-great grandfather
working away from home, only women folk were
left there alone. They knew it was on top of the
house.

Not knowing what to do, they built the
biggest fire they could in the fireplace to deter
the beast from crawling down the chimney.
Amidst the smoke and sparks, the painter leapt
from the house and perched itself high on the
hill. The story goes that the painter stayed there
and screamed through the whole birthing
process.

My great-great grandfather was born on
Rock Lick Creek in Jackson County, Kentucky
in the year of 1859.

The Wompus

By Ernest Hensley

((Reprinted from a student project *Harlan County Treasures*
with Judith Victoria Hensley at Wallins Elementary School and
Junior High in Harlan County, Kentucky)

I always heard about the old painter (panther) that was roaming around these mountains. Some folks called a painter "wompus." Some called him "Old Fairy."

You would hear him out there at night and hear him holler. He would make the eeriest sound. He sounded just like a woman screaming like she was being murdered or something awful happening to her.

People would say, "That's Old Fairy hollerin'!"

He got close to some people's house that lived up on the mountain. He started in to hollering. The man of the house got his rifle and went out there in the dark, looking for that painter. His name was Steve Hensley. He was out there in the dark a good long spell and finally they heard his rifle fire.

His family started saying, "He did it! Steve has shot Old Fairy!"

Sure enough, when he came back, he had killed Old Fairy, the wompus.

I've never actually seen a live panther except the ones they show on television, although the old people used to talk about them. It was not uncommon. To hear them scream at night was not uncommon.

I'm 86 now and I remember in my youth that one of our Hensley relatives came walking out of the Brush Mountain on the Kentucky/Virginia border with a big panther that he had killed. It was so big, he had to carry it around his shoulders. It was solid black. He had it wrapped around his shoulders and the nose still touched the ground!

I don't know how big of a man he was or how tall. But that took a big cat to lay around his shoulders with it's nose still touching the ground!

Credit: Adam Rifkin, via pandawhale.com/post/56720/a-black-jaguar-just-chilling and FLICKR

Native Americans and Black Panthers

(from Oral regional folklore)

By Judith Victoria Hensley

Oral history in the Appalachian Mountains often includes stories from Native Americans who inhabited the region before European Settlers arrived. It is my personal conviction that our ancestors spoke of the world around them and described things they saw which were common to their life experiences.

The stories they told about creatures of the forest were not meant to impress anyone this far into the future. They could have cared less what our current culture accepts or denies. From my perspective, the creatures they included in their stories were significant in their lives.

The panther was a creature common to Native American lore. The great Chief Tecumseh means, "panther passing across" in the Shawnee language. Tecumseh and his brother are best known for resisting the Europeans who were trying to get settled into the country.

Panthers were considered to be many things. In Native American folklore, the panther sometimes represents power. Sometimes it represents death. Sometimes it represents a powerful enemy. At other times, the sighting of a panther was considered to be a blessed event that marked the individual for greatness. Sightings or dreams of black panthers were often considered to be spiritual events. Black panther is one of several "clan animals."

The wampus/wompas (sometimes used to refer to a black panther) is a creature from early Cherokee folklore and also became part of the early American folklore. In Native American stories handed down, it is described as a horrible creature that is part human and part black panther. The wampus is often compared to other native big cats.

This creature was believed to be the result of a medicine man's curse on a Cherokee squaw who tried to disguise herself in a panther's skin and followed the braves to their secret ritual place. When she was discovered, the medicine man cursed her. She was doomed to wander the mountains forever. In one version of the tale, she was woman by day and panther by night.

In another story, a deer hunter hunts with a black panther. When the deer is taken, the panther invites him to join with other panthers for a feast. The man is welcomed in, but when he says he must go home, he is left alone in the cold and snow. When other hunters find him, he tells them the story, then dies within seven days, not content to be back among men.

In some folklore beliefs, the Wampus (or wompas) Cat is a spirit of death. When her cry is heard, it means someone is going to die and be buried within the next three days.

A Big Cat in Wallins

(Reprinted from a student project *from Harlan County and Its People* with Judith Victoria Hensley at Wallins Elementary School and Junior High in Harlan County, Kentucky)

By David Muncy

The last big cat I saw was about two weeks ago around the end of August or first part of September, 2011. I live at Wallins Creek, down across the river and the railroad tracks, down by the old welding building.

It was in the middle of the night and I heard something outside. I got my gun and went out to sit on the front porch and just listen and watch to see what was going on. There was nothing out of the ordinary that I could see. Two people walked past, but they weren't making any commotion.

I kept sitting there watching out into the darkness when I saw a big animal walking from the fire department. At first, I thought it was a great big yellow dog, but the longer I watched it, I knew it wasn't. It kept walking and came closer and closer, and finally down by my garden gate to where I had a perfect look at it.

It was no dog! It was a big old yellow mountain lion about the size of a large dog. It had a big long tail about three and a half feet long and big hair standing up around its neck. That cat had the most awful looking feet you ever saw in your life – as big as a man's fist or bigger.

I pulled my gun and shot into the ground over from that mountain lion. He turned and ran back up the holler toward the mountain. He sure took off when I fired my gun close to him.

That happened about 1:15 in the morning. I've not seen or heard anything else since then. I promise this is a true story and no joke.

Released into the **public domain** by its author, **Pearson Scott Foresman**.
Public domain image from Wikimedia commons

Happy Top

(Reprinted from a student project with Judith Victoria Hensley at Wallins Elementary School and Junior High in Harlan County, Kentucky)

By Karen Lindsey

One night early in spring, I was about to walk next door to see my mother when I got the shock of my life!

Earlier in the evening I had thrown some food scraps into the yard for my house cat to eat. The food was lying next to the stone pillars that adorn the sides of the walkway that leads to my porch. That is approximately ten feet from my front door.

The last time I looked, my cat was happily munching away.

As I started down the walk, heading for my mother's house, I had no idea what was waiting on the other side of one of the pillars. I walked down the sidewalk and had almost come to the end when I heard the slight noise of gravel being moved in the driveway. I looked to my right in the direction the sound came from.

What I saw scared me worse than I had ever been scared before!

My cat was still munching and totally oblivious to the fact that he was about to become dinner himself! Crouched down in a position to pounce on my poor unaware house cat was a young, very black (and I'm sure quite lethal) panther! My cat looked like a mouse compared to that big cat!

I froze. I couldn't get my mouth to scream or my legs to run! I just stood there like a statue, frozen in time. I stared at the panther and it stared back at me. Those large green eyes almost stopped my heart!

When I finally came to my senses, I turned, screaming at the top of my lungs, and ran toward my front door. I heard the panther move in the gravels as well.

Until I got into my house, I wasn't for sure if it was running away from me or toward me!

Thank the Lord, it ran back into the woods and my poor old cat had run into hiding somewhere.

Public Domain, Ghost of the Forest by Ranjith Kumar 2016 from Wikimedia Commons

Ginsenging

(Reprinted from a student project with Judith Victoria
Hensley at Wallins Elementary School and Junior High in Harlan
County, Kentucky)

By David Muncy

In the fall, I always go hunting for ginseng. I know some real good places to look for it up in these mountains. On one particular day in the fall of 2010, I had gone with a guy over into Whitley County. It was some time during September or October, I believe. That's the time of year to look for ginseng.

We had driven over into Whitley County to a place we knew that was a good spot to hunt for ginseng. We drove down Highway 130 toward Artemus, and then down to Brush Creek. It was a good day for ginsenging. The weather was cool, and the sun was shining.

It was about two hours before dark and we were still looking for ginseng on Brush Creek. We came around a bend and a big point in the mountain.

Right there in front of us was a huge old oak tree with a great big bottom limb about ten feet off the ground. Lying on that branch was a big yellow mountain lion sunning himself. He was beautiful. His fur was golden, and he had a big white chest.

He hadn't seen us, heard us, or smelled us as we approached because we were on the other side of the point, out of his sight. And we sure had not seen him, or had not expected to see him. We were all surprised to see each other!

He jumped down off of that limb and took off up into the woods. We stood still and watched him go. When we set out looking for ginseng that day, we sure didn't expect to come upon a mountain lion!

These stories I've told are real.

Public domain image from Wikimedia commons -
https://commons.wikimedia.org/wiki/User:CHUCAO

A Big Cat on the Bell County Line

(Reprinted from a student project with Judith Victoria Hensley at
Wallins Elementary School and Junior High in Harlan County,
Kentucky)

By David Muncy

People who have never seen a big cat in this part of the country claim there are none here. Officially, they say there are no mountain lions or panther in this region. People who have seen them know better.

There was this giant cat that was hit by a truck near the Harlan/Bell County line on Highway Kentucky 987 near Smith, Kentucky. The cat was accidentally hit by a truck as it ran across the road, but it was not killed – only seriously injured to where it couldn't run off.

The man who hit it didn't know what to do, so he called the Department of Fish and Wildlife. They came right away to try to help with the situation. The big cat was hurt too bad too run off, but he tried to charge one of the Fish and Game men while they were there trying to decide what they needed to do. The man had to shoot him and put him down.

The paws were gigantic. This big cat was pretty scary, but beautiful at the same time. It sure wasn't something a person would expect to run out in front of them driving down KY 987!

Begley Wildlife Management Area
By Judith Victoria Hensley

I hunt animals with my camera. I have thousands of photos to prove it. To me, there is nothing more relaxing and peaceful than being out in God's beautiful creation in search of scenery or animals in their natural habitat to photograph. I've had this hobby for decades. For me, it is something that never gets old and a good photo always makes me happy.

When I heard about an elk herd on Begley Wildlife Management Area on the Harlan County, Bell County Line of Straight Creek across Pine Mountain (Kentucky), I couldn't wait to go in search of elk. What I hadn't expected were the other animal encounters that happened while my friends and I were looking for elk.

One evening, Trish Halcomb and I had gone up to cruise the area in search of elk or a herd of wild horses. We always drive in a repeating pattern on the mountain roads. We had just finished one drive through and were getting ready to turn around at the sign that says "Increment #1."

Hunkered down was a big black object next to a bush right around the curve. We both saw it.

"It's a bear!" one of us said.

I had a camera in my hand and was trying to get it turned on when the creature stood up. It wasn't a bear! It was the biggest, blackest panther you can imagine!

There we sat, screaming, "Oh, my gosh! It's a panther!" while I was still waiting for my camera to give me the picture taking screen. With three or four big graceful bounds he was across the road and down the embankment out of sight.

Trish rolled her window down and sat on the opening with a camera in her hand, trying to see where the big cat had gone. No luck.

We decided that wasn't the brightest idea we'd ever had, either. That cat was bigger than a large German shepherd. If it was hiding and waiting to pounce on Trish while she was hanging out the window, she wouldn't have had a chance. That panther would have had her and drug her off into the underbrush before I could get my pistol out of its case.

That big black cat was beautiful. It looked like a picture from *Jungle Book*. Its body was sleek and solid black. Its tail was round and cylindrical, stretching out behind it as it ran.

Of course, when we told other people about it, they were skeptical. Some even laughed at us. Others wanted to know where the picture was. They couldn't comprehend how fast that big cat leaped across the road or what a shock it was to see one so unexpectedly.

I told my cousin, Rachel Johnson, about it. She sometimes keeps me company on my wildlife adventures. We went back up a few days later and were straining our eyeballs to catch sight of something. One day she saw a big yellow something on a side road. It was just sitting there and when it saw my little black car on the main road, it just rolled its head around to look at us, and then ran into the brush. We weren't sure if we had seen a big bobcat, a mountain lion, or maybe a coyote. It was too far to tell for sure with the naked eye.

We actually made several trips up the mountain together. We saw plenty of rabbit, lots of cat tracks, elk, wild horses, and a herd of cows, but no panther. One spring day we had just gotten up to the top of the mountain and were on our first drive through. At the high point we saw the herd of horses grazing in a field some distance away. We decided to drive the road behind them and try for a closer look.

Suddenly, Rachel pointed up to the right and said, "Look! What is that big black thing?"

I looked where she was pointing and there was a huge black cat, hunkered down in stealth mode just behind the ridge where we knew the horses were grazing. We watched it for a few seconds, its body taught, moving slow and close to the ground, and working its way silently toward the top of the ridge. There was no doubt about what it was or what it was doing. The unsuspecting horses on the other side of the ridge were about to have a surprise visitor.

We watched the big cat go over the crest of the hill like a deadly shadow. We were glad we didn't see what happened on the other side and hoped the horses had been able to outrun the hunter. We never saw it again that day.

Trish Halcomb wanted to take her daughter, Amber, back to see the wild horses and hoped to see the big cat again. Right at the edge of dark, Amber said she saw a panther over in the tall grass. Then Trish saw it.

I turned the car and shined my headlights into the grass where they were pointing. I didn't see anything, but they both said they did. They watched it for some time, sitting in the grass, staring at the headlights. They said it moved on a little further, then stopped again and turned its head back toward the headlights.

I couldn't see a thing, but I kept taking pictures in the direction they were pointing on the night photo setting of my camera. My own night vision is just not all that great. Later, when I put them up on the computer, there was no outline of a big cat in the photo, but there were two bright eyes shining back in every one of them.

I've made several other trips back up the mountain, but the elk have moved on, the horses are gone, and there aren't even any big cat tracks left for now. All that I've seen in the last few months up on Begley are a little herd of cows, rabbits, birds, and some small cat tracks that are probably from a bobcat.

I'll go back in the fall when the leaves have changed and see if the elk herd is back and the big cats with it.

R.G Badger, 1910

Back Yard Visitor
Author requests to remain anonymous

One day I was jumping on my trampoline outside my house and having fun all by myself. I heard an eerie screaming sound up on the mountain, but it only sounded once and was very far away. I didn't pay any attention to it at all.

I kept on jumping for a while, not really thinking about what might have made that scary sound up on the mountain, when suddenly, a panther just came out of nowhere. There it stood right in my yard! I saw its eyes and we just locked eyes on each other.

It was huge and solid black. I was too afraid to even move and couldn't even think straight. It was only a few feet away from where I was standing on the trampoline. I had not heard it come out of the woods. I had been jumping and not paying attention to anything else at all. So, there I stood on my trampoline, without a clue of what I should do and scared to death to move or scream for help.

My husky must have sensed that I was in danger, because he broke his chain where he was chained to the doghouse and came running. I think he sensed my terror.

My dog came running toward us as fast as his legs would carry him and barking his head off. He jumped right on that panther!

My dog is big. He's a Husky, but the panther was bigger. The panther clamped down around his neck but didn't really hurt him. The panther let him go and just turned around and ran off. It was really fast!

After it ran across my yard, my dog was still barking. I grabbed his leash and didn't let him run after the panther. All of the neighborhood dogs started barking. I guess they saw it, smelled it, or sensed it being there.

I was too scared to tell my parents or anything. I was afraid they wouldn't believe me, and if they did, I might never get to go outside and play again!

I have never seen or heard the panther scream again since then. Now that I know what they sound like, I listen to make sure I don't ever hear one again on that mountain! If I ever do, I will get my dog and stand on the porch. If I ever see one again, I will try to stay calm and sic my dog on it!

Panther Surprise

By Trish Halcomb

I had been with a friend on Pine Mountain driving around on a strip job where we had often seen animals in the past. We have seen rabbits, snakes, a baby bear, deer, elk, birds, wild horses, cows, and all kinds of animal tracks.

We decided it was time to leave the mountain around dusky dark. We had not seen much of anything that day. We got to the end of one section of gravel road and started to turn left to go off of the mountain on the main gravel road which is very, very wide. It has to be for the big equipment to be taken in up to the mining site.

About ten yards down the road to the left, in the direction we were starting to turn, we saw some kind of big black animal hunkered down beside of an olive berry bush. We thought it was a bear and we were excited about that. We were both staring at it and trying to figure out for sure if it was a bear and how big it was.

Both of us had cameras in our hand, but it would have been hard to get a photo right at the edge of dark. It was still light enough that we could see the road clearly and the shape of the animal hunkered down there.

We turned the car and shined the headlights in that direction. When the animal stood up, the first thing I noticed was that it had a long, round, tail and the whole thing was as black as night.

It was a solid black panther! In about two or three big leaps, it had crossed that whole big wide mining road. By the time we realized what it was, it was gone out of sight over the bank on the other side of the road into the woods.

We hadn't even had time to turn our cameras on, much less take a photo.

Of course, nobody will believe a story about a panther unless they have seen one for themselves. I told my family and a few people. Some found it hard to believe and others had seen things themselves or heard stories.

A few days later I decided to take my daughter back up there to see if we might catch a glimpse of that panther and prove, at least to her, that it was real. She is one of those people that has to see it to believe it.

We were about half of a mile past the place where we spotted the panther a few nights before. It was almost too dark to see, and once again, we were about to turn around and leave the mountain. Amber saw the panther first.

When the car's headlights hit on that big black cat's eyes, they glowed in the dark.

We watched it in the tall grass and turned the car so the headlights were shining right on the panther. We could see it turn its head and every once in a while, it would blink. It moved a few feet, sat back down, and stared at the lights.

We watched it for about ten or fifteen minutes and thought we might have seen another set of eyes on back in the weeds, but weren't sure about that. We were sure of the one the headlights were shining on, even though it blended into the darkness. We would have missed it if Amber hadn't caught sight of it before it got too dark.

Kentucky Wildcat photo by Judith Victoria Hensley

Big Cats at Tremont
By D. Blanton

(Reprinted from a student project with Judith Victoria Hensley at Wallins Elementary School and Junior High in Harlan County, Kentucky)

For the past week or so, our dog has been barking for no reason. Well, maybe it was for a reason. We just didn't realize what it was!

One morning while my brother and I were standing at the bus stop, we looked back at this old swinging bridge that crosses the river by Pine Flat Baptist Church. We saw a black figure walking across the bridge. I thought it was a dog at first.

As it stepped clearly into the light, I saw that it was not a dog. It was a black panther. Its face was kind of strange. It came out in the front and was more squarish or rectangular than a dog's face.

There is a house right beside of the bridge and four little kittens were out in the yard. When that big cat came across the bridge, they ran straight to the porch. The panther walked over behind them, like it was following them to the porch. The panther was humongous compared to the kittens.

It walked across the porch and jumped off the end just as the bus was coming. It went around the back of that house to where we couldn't see it any more as we were getting on the bus. We were about fifty yards away when we saw it.

Last fall on September 21, 2011, my dad and I were down by the riverbank fishing at Tremont, Kentucky. The fish were not biting very well. We caught a couple of fish but had to throw them back. The water in that creek is contaminated because of the factory that used to be at Dayhoit. But fishing is fun, even if you don't eat the fish and let them go.

There was a big beaver across the river smacking its tail at us and trying to run us off. A tree had just fallen about a week before where the beaver cut it down with its teeth. It was busy taking off the branches and it did not want us there.

We started hearing twigs snapping across the river. It was obvious that something big was over there besides the busy beaver. My dad turned on his mining light and shined it over there to see if it was a deer or a bear. That's what he thought it was going to be.

It wasn't anything that we would have been expecting. When the light hit it, it shined on two big mountain lions. One was walking in front and the other following behind.

They were a dark orangish yellow color and their faces were shaped like a big square. Their whole bodies had no fat on them. They were solid muscle. You could see the muscles moving throughout their body, especially in their shoulders, whenever they went to take a step. They were huge!

They walked on down the river and down the bank to a place where there are rocks and the river isn't so deep. They were crossing the river.

My dad and I grabbed up everything we had and started walking home, getting out of there. We could hear them making weird noises and splashing around in the river. We aren't sure what they were doing, but we think they were catching fish. The fish had been splashing around at the top of the water eating bugs, but they weren't biting for us. My dad had tried to take a picture when they were on the other side of the river, but the flash only showed the weeds closest to us. The distance was too far and the weeds that showed up just covered up the two big mountain lions.

We were really hoping the pictures would turn out. Even if you couldn't have seen the whole big cats, we were hoping you could see at least the outline of the mountain lions to get an idea of how big they were.

My dad said they were about three feet tall, but he couldn't tell how long they were. The way their bodies were angled away from us across the river, he just couldn't say how long they would have been. We just knew they were big!

Martins Fork Panther

By Judith V. Hensley

Here's the thing about seeing a panther. If you see one, you will never forget it and you can go right back to almost the exact spot where it happened. It is burned into your mind like some earth changing event. People remember where they were on 9/11 when the planes hit the Twin Towers. If they are old enough, most people remember where they were when news came that President John F. Kennedy had been assassinated. Seeing a black panther evokes the same response.

I realize that the state biologist, the Department of Fish and Wildlife, and every other official government employee or agency in the state of Kentucky will say that there are no black panthers in Kentucky or anywhere else in Appalachia. They say there is no separate species of black cat such as the type people describe. I have been openly scoffed at for saying that I have seen one.

Scoff or not, I know what I've seen. As a matter of fact, I have been very fortunate through my lifetime to have seen a panther on more than one occasion. The first one I ever saw instead of heard was in McCreary County, Kentucky. Almost two decades passed before I saw another one.

It was the first week of December in 1988. My son and I lived in Martin's Fork, Kentucky with my parents at that time. I had driven home from work and was taking my mother back out to town to go Christmas shopping. It was already very dark.

We were almost at the Martin's Fork Dam when my headlights flashed on something shiny on a ledge on the righthand side of the road. I looked and there sat a magnificent black panther sitting on the rocks as if it were posing for a painting. It rolled its head toward us and blinked a couple of times but didn't flinch even a muscle anywhere else. Its long tail was wrapped around its feet and hung down on the ledge with the tip of it moving slightly.

I pointed and yelled for my mom to look, but she had no idea what I was talking about. We passed within 20-30 feet of it.

The whole sighting only lasted a few seconds before we went around the bend in the road. I couldn't see anything in my rearview mirror. To this day, I don't know why I didn't turn around and go back or just put my car in reverse and see if it was still sitting there after we passed.

I drove out to work every week day morning around 6:30 a.m. It was pitch black in the winter months. One morning a black panther ran across the road in front of the car

between the old Post Office and the Riverside
Baptist Church. Its muscles rippled as it
moved. and it didn't look like it had an ounce of
fat anywhere on its body. The long cylindrical
tail bobbed behind as it ran.

That location is only a couple or three
miles from where I had seen a panther sitting
on the ledge. I started watching for it every
morning and every night on the way to and from
work.

One other time I got a glimpse of a big
black something jumping over the hill and into
a ditch before I got to the Riverside Church, but
I didn't get a good enough look at the head to be
sure if it was maybe the panther or maybe a big
black dog. I couldn't say for sure.

I never saw anything else down that
stretch of road again.

Decades later, in the last couple of years, I
saw another one on the top of Pine Mountain in
the Begley Wildlife Management Area, which I
have also written about for this book.

It doesn't make one bit of difference to me
whether anybody else ever believes me or not
when it comes to having seen a black panther.
I've never seen a tawny colored one close
enough to be absolutely sure that's what it was,
but I definitely have seen the black ones.

I still hold out hope that someone in the
region will finally get a photograph of a black
panther, a mountain lion, or find one that's

been hit on the road, get a video of one, or
footprints that are clear enough to be accepted
by the authorities. Basically, the message is
that until they have absolute proof, they will
never acknowledge the presence of black
panthers or big cats in Kentucky or in
Appalachia.

Photos by Judith V. Hensley, Southeastern Kentucky-Adult shoe
size 8

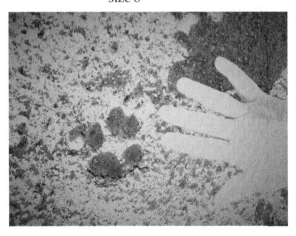

She Cat (A Tall Tale)

Told by and in Memory of the Late

Jim Roark

Reprinted from a Wallins Elementary Student Project with
Judith Victoria Hensley – *Harlan County at Its Best*, 1993

About a hundred years ago at Pathfork, Kentucky there were only a few people living on the mountain. There were only three houses and they were very far apart.

A new family moved to the mountain and they had a little boy that was about twelve years old and a little girl about nine years old. Their momma sent them out together blackberry picking one day. Well, it started getting on up in the evening and the children didn't come home. The woman knew something bad was wrong. They knew better to stay gone until after dark. The mountains were full of wild things that hunted at night.

The man and woman rounded up people far and near to help look for their children. They didn't find them all that night. They looked for them all the next day, as well. When they did find something, it was only their shoes. They were up near this old lady's house who lived alone. They asked her about the children and the shoes. She said, no, she hadn't seen two children up that way.

t went on a little while and they still hadn't found anything out about those children.

There was another family on the mountain who owned some cattle. They started finding some of their cattle dead and partly eaten. They had big claw marks on them where they had been ripped open. The people knew then that it was probably a panther that was getting everything.

They all got out and started hunting. They hunted everywhere around and couldn't find any sign of a panther. So they decided that the only way to catch a panther was at night. They all got out and got their dogs to help them hunt for that panther.

They started up by the old woman's house and told her what they were doing and where they would be hunting, so as not to scare her. She thanked them for letting her know exactly where they would be.

They hunted all that night and didn't see a thing. The next night, all the men got out and they went another place. They didn't go up the same way by the old lady's house. After they had been hunting until about 1:00 or 2:00 in the morning, they heard a panther scream. It was really loud, as loud as they'd ever heard. It almost scared the men to death. They said it made their blood curdle, it was so loud!

All of their dogs came running to them and just laid down at their feet and whimpered, scared to death! They didn't find any sign of anything that night – only heard it.

The men started not to hunt any more, but the man who had lost his little boy and little girl said he was going even if he had to go by himself. Some of the men decided they would go back with him the next night and try to help. They went back to the same place where they had heard the panther screaming the night before. They heard it again.

That night they had taken some more dogs with them that were bear dogs. That panther screaming didn't scare those bear dogs too bad. They got to running that panther and finally the men caught sight of it! They said it was the biggest, blackest panther any of them had ever seen in their lives!

They all started shooting at it and one of them saw that he had hit it. It fell right in front of them. They ran over to where it was at and it was lying there dying. They said it was a huge black panther.

All at once they said it started shrinking! It turned into that old woman who lived by herself up on the mountain!

The old woman really was a She Cat and she was the one who had been chasing things down and killing them for many a year. They thought of all the livestock that had been found over the years, missing people that no one ever knew what had happened to them, and that man's little boy and girl who had gone out blackberry picking and never came home.

That old She Cat had roamed the
mountains for years disguised as an old woman
by day and turning into her real self by night!

*Wikimedia commons public domain image by Bruce McAdams,
Reykjavic, Iceland, August 28, 2009*

Panther Stories in My Family

By J. Hawkins as told by Emily Turner

(Reprinted from a student project with Judith Victoria
Hensley at Wallins Elementary School and Junior High in Harlan
County, Kentucky)

My uncle, Tim Hawkins, and his wife, Billie, live in Fresh Meadows, Kentucky. Their house is before you get to the Dayhoit Bridge. There is a cut off before the bridge and you turn to the right to go to their house.

The neighbors had been telling about seeing a big black panther in the neighborhood. They had heard it scream and some had actually seen it. My uncle wasn't too sure about it.

He decided to put a trail camera up behind Mamaw's house (Barbara Hawkins) by the screen door to see if anything was out there in her yard. He figured if anything was lurking around, maybe it would pass by the camera. He didn't get anything on the trail cam at first.

One day, he saw the panther in real life standing in Mamaw's yard. It was very close to where he was standing, maybe twenty feet. When the panther saw him, it ran away.

My uncle decided to track it. He followed the panther's paw prints to an abandoned house that is right up above my Mamaw's house. There is a road and some woods that separate that house from Mamaw. The panther was living in the basement of that house. It had two cubs!

The big black mother panther was solid black, and so was one of the babies. But the other cub was brown.

They started keeping an eye out for the big cat coming and going. She must have taken up residence in the abandoned house to have her babies. The people who had moved out left the basement door wide open when they moved.

When people saw her roaming, she was probably looking for food.

Tim saw the panther one more time behind his house. His neighbor's dogs scared it off.

Many of the neighbors' cats went missing. They would suddenly vanish without a trace. It is possible that the panther was getting them for food. None of the missing housecats have ever been found.

The panther must have sensed that people had found her hide away. She took her cubs and disappeared from that old abandoned house. No one has seen her for a while.

On another occasion, my Aunt Emily was home alone. She was cooking supper. She heard soft footsteps upstairs in her house, like someone pacing back and forth. She knew no one was up there and it frightened her.

She called Uncle Tim to come and check for her, because she is in a wheelchair and was unable to go up there herself. He came down and checked out the entire house. He didn't find a sign of anything or anyone, so he tried to assure her that the house was empty and finally left.

She was certain that she heard the footsteps, even if he didn't find anything. She kept watching and actually saw a panther jump off of the roof of her house. She realized the footsteps she heard pacing back and forth had been on the roof as the panther paced. It was a good thing my uncle didn't find it!

Apparently, the big black cat had smelled the food she was cooking and had been trying to find a way to get in the house.

Another time my other aunt, Shirley, was baking a ham for Christmas. She placed the ham in the oven before going to bed so the meat would bake slowly all night and be tender and delicious on Christmas Day.

Around 2:00 a.m. she heard something hit her trailer. Then she heard footsteps pacing back and forth over the entire length of the trailer. She didn't know what to do! She listened, and the footsteps continued.

Finally, she decided to wake her husband. She told him what had happened, and he listened, too.

He got his gun and went outside. He walked out into the yard far enough to be able to see the top of their trailer and try to figure out what was up there.

A big black panther was standing on top of their trailer! When the big cat saw him, it jumped off the trailer and ran into the woods.

That panther must have decided that the smell of that baking ham was my aunt's way of inviting him to Christmas dinner! My uncle standing in the yard with a gun in his hand must have been his idea of getting uninvited!

That was the only time they ever saw or heard the panther near that trailer.

1843- England, Vintage Public Domain Image

Family Story

By Roger Glynn Richardson

My family passes down a story about my great-grandfather. He had been visiting his gal and was coming back home. A "painter" jumped across the horse he was riding on.

Blood Curdling Screams

By Charles Stacy Prince

I live in Polk County, Tennessee. I've never seen a panther, but when I was a teenager, a buddy and I were walking up the driveway out of the holler just after dark, when we heard this blood curdling scream about twenty feet away. It sounded like a woman and a baby screaming at the same time.

It scared the crap out of us! We turned around and ran back home.

I've heard people say they've seen black panthers around here. I haven't seen one, but surely might have heard one.

Something in the Shed

By H. Smith

(Reprinted from a student project with Judith Victoria Hensley at Wallins Elementary School and Junior High in Harlan County, Kentucky)

I looked out the window at Mamaw Buell's house and saw leaves blowing off the trees and across the yard. It looked like it was raining leaves of all different colors. The mountains were orange, brown, gold, and red.

My cousin, Brandon Buell, was looking in a horse shed down from my Granny's house. I could see him out the corner of the window. All of a sudden, I heard him scream.

"Haylee!" he screamed. I knew something was wrong.

He flew up toward my Granny's on foot and as he was running toward the house I saw a terrified look on his face. I heard an unearthly scream like a woman. It sounded like the woman was being murdered, like a painful scream. Then I heard another scream like the loud crying of a baby.

My Granny came running in there screaming at us, "What in the world are you all doing? What is going on in here? Is someone hurt?"

The door was open, and Brandon was standing on the steps looking back toward the shed. "No, Granny! Nobody's hurt," I said.

Brandon said, "Granny, there is someone in the shed screaming like a woman getting murdered, and there is a baby screaming in there with her!"

"Oh, no!" my Granny exclaimed. She said, "It might be a panther."

Brandon jumped inside the house and slammed the door shut and locked it.

It scared me to death. It sounded just like a woman getting murdered and it was coming closer to the house. What if it really was a woman in pain? OR what if it really was a panther?

I said, "Granny! What are we going to do? What if it comes up here?"

Brandon called down to his mom's house and told them, "DO NOT GO OUTSIDE! There is something or someone in the shed and it might be a panther. It sounds just like a woman screaming or in pain."

Eventually that awful screaming stopped. Granny kept watching the shed to see if anyone or anything came out while Brandon got his nerve up and got Papaw Sam's shotgun and went down there. My Papaw Sam died last year, and Brandon was doing what Papaw would have done if he was still alive.

I was too scared to watch. I ran in Granny's bedroom and got in her closet! I heard a gunshot and then another scream. There were two screams close together and another different loud scream like it was answering back to the first one.

Then I heard another gunshot. I had my fingers in my ears. The screams and the shots like to have scared me to death.

Granny hollered, "Here comes Brandon. Haylee, you can come out now! He's okay."

He said he had looked in the shed and saw something big and black moving in the corner of the shed. He couldn't make out what it was, but it was a big animal. And he could hear the screams. He shot into the darkness toward the movement. There was a light inside of that shed, but he was too scared to put his hand in there and turn it on.

After he shot, he turned around and ran back to the house. He was afraid something was going to come out of there and get after him! We decided we'd better all stay in the house and leave whatever it was alone. Maybe it would go away by itself if no one bothered it.

Later that night when Brandon's dad, Paul Buell went out on the porch to have a smoke, he heard something in the woods breaking branches and stuff in the woods behind their house. He said it sounded just like somebody walking around up there, breaking tree branches and snapping twigs. He saw a black shape going across the yard and back up into

the woods. It was too dark to be sure what it
was. He said it was black and he could see the
outline of its ears, but he couldn't be sure of
what it was.

The Mountain Cat

(Reprinted from a student project with Judith Victoria
Hensley at Wallins Elementary School and Junior High in Harlan
County, Kentucky)

By A. Duncan

About five years ago in the fall of 2006, my
mom, brother, sister, and I had an encounter
that none of us will ever forget. We were living
at Cumberland at the time but went to church
in Evarts. To save time and gas, Mom would
drive across Slope Holler instead of going
through Harlan and all the way back around.

It was a cool autumn evening and we
started the drive back across the mountain. It
was getting dusky as we headed home, and I
was looking forward to playing a game before
bed.

We had made this same trip together
dozens of times before, but this time across
Slope Holler was different. I remember
watching the woods by the road as we passed
by. Sometimes we watched just so we might get
a glimpse of a deer or a bear.

Once we even saw an owl. When we stopped to get a closer look, he just stared at us for a while before he flew off.

You just never know what you might see if you pay attention going across Slope Holler.

I continued to watch and suddenly mom hit the brakes and our Jeep came to a screeching halt. She screamed out, "Did you see that?"

I hadn't seen what she was talking about, but whatever it was, it had her shaking. She said she had seen the tail end of a big black cat. It bolted across the road and into the woods as we came around the curve. She said that all she could make out was its hind legs and a long tail as long as she stood tall.

We weren't scared because we knew it was running away and it couldn't get through the windows of the car to get to us. So we went on down the mountain until we came to another steep curve and Mom stopped the Jeep again.

There was a huge branch lying across the road. At first mom didn't know what to do, but then she put the Jeep in park and set the emergency brake. I didn't know what she was doing, but when she opened the door to get out, I got scared.

She told me to stay in the car with my brother and sister while she moved the branch. I did what she told me to do, but I was afraid that whatever my mom had seen was coming to get her.

It felt like forever before she got the branch moved. I watched her struggle with it. I wanted to help her, but she told me to stay put. Finally, she came running back to the car and she just sat there shaking and quiet.

I asked her if she was scared, but she said that she wasn't. I knew that she was truly scared, but I was just glad to finally be on our way home again.

We got home without further incident and told Dad about it the next day. He said that he never wanted Mom driving across Slope Holler again, but she did. It was still the fastest way between church and home.

Creative Commons Image - Rich Beausoleil, WDFW - From: No Place for Predators? Gross L PLoS Biology Vol. 6, No. 2

Black Panther and My Malibu

By Ricky Skidmore

(Taped Interview from Harlan County Story Telling Festival
2017)

I've seen one panther when I was younger
– in my twenties. It was in the fall of the year,
about eighteen years ago.

I was working for Secure X between
Holmes's Mill, Kentucky and the Virginia line,
up on what's called 6C on Lone Mountain at a
guard shack. I used to drive an old '76 Malibu
that was solid white. I had parked and
positioned the car that night so that the light
would shine on the car, so I could see if anyone
came up or was messing with my car.

I was in the guard shack and I kept
hearing noises outside. I'd go to the window
and look out to try to see what was making the
noise and I could see anything at all. While I
was watching, I was looking over towards my
car. I saw this head start to creep around
towards my front wheel. It kept moving slowly
along until it stretched out and got to my back
wheel. It was in the shape and form of a
panther. With the body beside of the car, the
tail still wrapped around the back a little bit. It
kind of flicked it around.

The next morning, I measured the distance between my front wheel and my back wheel after seeing this. The distance between was about eight feet long. From the head to the butt, that was from the front wheel to the back wheel, and its tail wrapped around. I could tell plainly what it was. There was and is no doubts in my mind.

I did not want to go outside in the middle of the night after that. People say they don't exist, but I KNOW they exist.

On a Coal Mining Strip Job Road

By Allyson Asher Caldwell

(Taped interview from Harlan County Story Telling Festival 2017)

I was riding on a strip job with my husband, George and there was snow on the ground. We saw the black panther against the white snow and it was plain to tell what it was.

It had a long tail that kind of swooped up at the end. I got excited and told him to stop, so he did. He stopped right in the middle of this little bend we had been driving around. The panther ran off and we never saw it again.

My husband worked on that strip job. There were several different reports from the

people who worked there on that strip site of of
people who had seen a panther there right in
that same area.

Jumping Like Rainbow Arches
(Reprinted from a student project with Judith Victoria
Hensley at Wallins Elementary School and Junior High in Harlan
County,)
By Elizabeth Hamlin

I have hiked all through these woods ever
since we moved back here to Corbin, Kentucky
from Michigan. We were always careful and
watched out for things, wild animals you know,
but the biggest things we were concerned about
were poison snakes or maybe a wild dog.

The trails have bears on them these days.
One time a bear came to my sister's house and
was eating the dog food. The dog was trying his
best to scare the bear away. It would climb up
the tree near their deck, and then come back
down. It did that several times with that dog
trying to protect its food. Finally, it gave up and
went away.

It didn't come back for a few nights. My
sister heard a shot one night and wondered if
somebody might have shot that bear, or at least
scared it enough not to come back around
people's houses.

One day we were walking, and a big bear
crossed the creek right in front of us. I've gotten

afraid of being out in the woods more than I ever use to be.

One time, my husband Robert was gone to my brother Leon's and I decided I'd go for a walk alone. I love to walk in the woods. I decided I'd better take my nephew's dogs with me. They are good dogs and they love to get turned loose in the woods.

We were walking down by the creek and I saw this big black thing running out in front. At first, I thought it was one of the dogs. It was looked like the big black dog from a distance but seemed a little bigger. It was jumping as it ran in arches like rainbows. I had never seen a dog do that before. It was a beautiful motion, just like he was making rainbows.

It went down the holler. I was following along down that way, still thinking it was a dog. I got plenty close enough to see it.

It crossed a log over the stream in plain view. Then I knew it wasn't a dog. I could tell by the steady way it went across that log, very sure footed. A dog will kind of hesitate and pick its way across a downed log over a creek. This big black thing was sure footed and casual about it. It never hesitated at all. I saw the muscles rippling and the big long rounded tail trailing out behind and I could tell for sure that it was a panther. It went very steadily across that log.

I had never seen a panther before in my life – just on animal shows on TV. I never expected to see anything like that in the woods around here. (Corbin, Kentucky just off the Cumberland Falls Highway). It was beautiful, and all, but it really shook me up. It scared me so badly I turned and headed back out of the woods as fast as I could go – me and the dogs. And there was that big black dog sticking with me and the rest of the dogs that I had mistaken in the place of the panther.

I sure was glad to get back to the house. Between seeing bears and seeing that panther, I am very cautious about just going for a walk in the woods alone. It's not at all like it used to be, when you felt safe, before people started seeing all these things.

Fairview, North Carolina

By Jean Reese

Many years ago (maybe 20-30), the newspaper in Fairview, North Carolina ran a picture of one that had attacked a calf out in the pasture.

I saw a big mountain lion myself on Arrowhead Mountain in Fairview. Also, when I was walking early one morning, I saw one around 7:00, about three times. I knew where his cave was.

Panther Found

(Reprinted from a student project with Judith Victoria
Hensley at Wallins Elementary School and Junior High in Harlan
County,) Kentucky)

By B. Jones

About a year ago, my brother and I were walking out on the porch, and we heard this odd noise, as if a woman were screaming. We looked all about the yard and didn't see anything. When we looked over the rail and at the bottom of our porch, which is about 10 feet off the ground, was this big black animal just standing there. It appeared to be a black panther. I don't think it saw us or realized we were there at first because we were so high off the ground and it was down on the hill.

We both ran inside to get a camera. I got my camera and my brother got his. His did not work. I hurried and got back out on the porch and it was still there. I took a snapshot. The panther turned and started walking down the driveway. I was terrified. It looked back over its shoulder at us and we went back inside. The panther went on down the hill.

I got a total of three photos, but only one was good enough to really tell what it was.

The people who work for the Department of Fish and Wildlife say there are no panthers in Kentucky or in Harlan County. So, my brother called them and told them what we had seen and that I had a photo of the panther.

They came to our house. I took my camera out and said, "Tell me again that there are no panthers living in Harlan County!"

The guy had no clue what to say.

The Wildlife Manager asked for our number. If we saw the panther again, we could call them. I gave them our number and the next night I was calling them because the panther was back in the yard.

I was outside shooting basketball and I saw it again behind our storage building. I ran straight in the house and called.

My brother, Mark, and I were sitting in the living room watching the television when we heard a car pulling in. We walked out to see who it was and were surprised to see that it was the Wildlife people. They said they were going to set up a video camera to see the panther.

They came back the next night to get their camera. We all sat down and watched the video in our house. It turned out that the panther was pregnant. In the video the panther was leaving. She must have gone somewhere else to have her baby.

I'm not sure it was the same panther in the video that we saw because the first one was skinny and the one in the video looked very fat.

After that we haven't seen the panther since. We didn't hear anything else from the Department of Fish and Wildlife either. They still claim there are no black panthers in Kentucky – even after we gave them the proof that there is. It kind of makes me wonder what else they know about and are not telling.

We have not seen any more panthers in our yard or around our property, but we have seen black bears.

Photo by Judith Victoria Hensley – Kentucky Wildcat, Salato Center, Frankfort, Kentucky

I asked to see the photo mentioned in this story or to use it in with the student's story for the project, but someone had borrowed it and had not returned it

Panther

By M. Howard

(Reprinted from a student project with Judith Victoria Hensley at
Wallins Elementary School and Junior High in Harlan County,
Kentucky)

Walking through the woods, a blanket of
white fog covered the air. I was on a quest with
one of my dad's work buddies to cut some
timbers down for a quick sale at the saw mill
and wasn't paying attention to where I was
walking. Never in a million years did we dream
that we were in for the surprise that was just
ahead.

As I began cutting a large tree down, a
roaring screaming sound echoed through the
mountainside. I quickly stopped the power saw
and looked over my right shoulder where the
sound had come from. I saw nothing there.

The guy who was with me was sitting on a
log waiting for me to get the tree down so we
could pack it out.

I looked behind me and saw a panther
coming toward me from another direction. It
must have been the mate of the first one that I
heard. We started to run and saw a tree with
low branches. That panther was right behind
us. We hit the tree and went straight to the top
away from the panther. The tree was flimsy and
the panther didn't try to climb up after us.

We saw them both. They were big – about the size of a German shepherd.

We just clung there, waiting for the panthers to go away. They circled the tree, then sat down and stared up at us, like they knew we'd have to come down sooner or later.

I heard a voice in the distance. It was my dad walking toward us. First he saw us up in the top of that tree hanging on and knew there was something wrong. He saw the panthers and his immediate reaction was to try to kill them. He pulled his pistol out and shot at them.   They ran off.

We climbed down out of the tree and went back for our chainsaw. We saw another one, or one of the same ones, but this time it ran away from us.

We finished cutting the tree and left.

That was the scariest moment of my life when I saw that big black panther coming toward me and there I was with no gun or anything for protection.

(Traditionally in Harlan County, Kentucky when someone says they've seen a panther, painter, or wompus they are referring to the solid black cats which are the same size as the yellow cats that people call mountain lions or cougars. The only difference is the color. With the more frequent sightings of these big yellow cats, some people have begun to also refer to them as panthers.)

Big Cat on a Turkey Hunt

By Johnny Baker

(Reprinted from a student project with Judith Victoria
Hensley at Wallins Elementary School and Junior High in Harlan
County, Kentucky)

It was a spring day in 2003. It was a beautiful day for hunting turkey with the sun shining and a brisk light breeze blowing. I had decided to try my luck on the ridge between Laurel Branch and Big Branch in Harlan County, Kentucky.

I was alone on the mountain and decided to go to the little saddle at the top of the mountain that dips down and back up, providing a great view. You can see that very place if you are driving down Highway 119 on the Molus Straight and look up at the power line right where the dip is. I was sitting in the saddle with my back up against a cedar tree to give me cover. I was completely under the branches. I sat facing down Big Branch.

There was a turkey out there gobbling and answering back every call I made. It was slowly moving closer toward me. I could tell it by the turkey's calls. I was watching for the turkey to come into sight when I caught a movement out of the corner of my eye.

I looked in that direction and saw a big cat coming down the road toward ME. It was coming toward me stealthily, crouching and inching steadily forward. I had been making such believable turkey calls, that the cat thought I WAS THE TURKEY!

I kept watching the cat coming toward me and I thought to myself, "That's the biggest bobcat I have ever seen in my life!"

I watched it come toward me for another forty or fifty yards before I realized it wasn't a bobcat. It was a mountain lion! I knew it when I saw the big three to four-foot long tail sweeping out behind it as it inched closer. Its body was three to four feet long from nose to end and the tail was at least that long again behind it. Bobcats have short stumpy tails. This cat was a dirty yellow color and was nothing I'd ever seen before.

At the moment I realized what it was, it startled me so bad, that I jerked. My movement caused the cedar branches over me to shake. The cat stopped and stared straight at the tree – straight at ME for about three to five seconds.

I imagine the cat was surprised when he realized I was no turkey. It turned, and with about three long jumps back up the mountain, it was gone out of sight. It moved so fast, I realized that if it had decided to come at me instead of away, there wouldn't even have been time for me to raise my gun, much less take aim, and make an accurate shot that would have brought the big cat down.

I sat for a minute or two, thought about what had happened, jumped back on my four-wheeler and tore out of there for home with the real turkey still gobbling somewhere close by.

I do a lot of turkey hunting. I sometimes go over into Brownie's Creek to the place they call The Playground. I also go hunting in Liggett and Pathfork for grouse. I've seen a lot of different animals, including multiple bobcat sightings. But I have never, ever seen anything the size of that cat.

Wikimedia Commons public domain image by Manfred Werner at the Salzburg Zoo, January 30, 2014

Panther in the Back Yard

By D. Lamb

(Reprinted from a student project with Judith Victoria
Hensley at Wallins Elementary School and Junior High in Harlan
County, Kentucky)

I live on Cedar Street in Loyall, Kentucky. Our backyard backs right up to the river. I was out playing football in the back yard yesterday, November 19, 2011 even though it was drizzling rain. I am a football player.

Something caught my eye at the corner of the house. When I looked, it was a huge black cat, about the size of a German shepherd but shaped differently. Its face was different and its ears. Its back would have easily come up to the girdle of my football uniform.

The big cat had come from the front of my house around to the back yard. It wasn't doing anything but looking at me when I heard what sounded like smaller cats making some weird noise like yowling or half way roaring, but I couldn't see them.

Then two smaller solid black cats came around the corner of the house and stood by the big cat, which I guess was their mother. They would have come up to my knees probably. They just stood there beside of her, staring at me.

It nearly scared me to death! I ran straight in the house and told Mom, but I don't think she believed me. I went in my bedroom and looked out the window. All three of them, the mother and two babies were going up the hill behind my house toward the river.

I don't think I'll ever go back out there and play football by myself.

This morning when I went to the bus, I saw big muddy tracks by the R. C. Plant and I wondered if they belonged to that huge mother cat. The R. C. Plant is by the railroad tracks where I catch the bus. Across the tracks are grown up fields, the river, and the mountain.

When I came to school and told my teacher, she asked me what kind of cat it was. I didn't know. I looked at some pictures she had and found one that looked just like it. It was a panther.

My Mamaw lives on that mountain and I'm going to warn her today. I'll tell my Papaw to keep an eye out for them, too. I never saw a cat so big and black as that mother cat.

Public Domain image by Dheeraj pach in uttrakhand green forest September 26, 2011

What My Granny Saw
By Misty Brock

Granny was sitting on her porch drinking coffee around 10:00 p.m. one summer night. She heard something in her back yard and got up to see what it was. She has a little yard with bushes and stuff in it. That's what she heard swishing around and making the noises.

She thought it was her son, but it wasn't. "Willie? Is that you?" she hollered.

No one answered, and she continued to call his name. Still nobody answered. She still heard the noise, so she got a little closer to where the noise was coming from.

She thought maybe Willie was trying to scare her as a joke. She thought he might be hiding in the bushes and going to jump out and holler, "Boo!" at her.

"Well," she thought to herself, "if that is him trying to scare me, he's doing a good job!" It was not Uncle Willie.

She was almost at the source of the noise when something black stood up and walked away. It had been lying under the bushes eating something. There are wild turkeys around her house, so she thought whatever it was might have caught a turkey and been eating it.

In the darkness, she really couldn't tell what it was, but she had frightened it off.

She went back to the front porch and had a seat with her coffee. She heard the noise again a little while later. Since she knew it was some sort of animal, and thought it probably was a stray dog. She didn't bother to go looking for it again. She really didn't care about a stray being out there, as long as it wasn't a human messing around.

She saw a movement in the dark. The black thing was walking across the yard. It had come from the back yard, circled around the garage and was walking toward the house. Right there in front of her face, she finally realized what it was – a black panther!

She ran into the house and locked the door behind her! She said she got her camera out and tried to take a picture through the window in the door, but we have never seen the picture. It might not have turned out because if it flashed on the glass, it would have just been a reflection of the flash. She stood there and watched to see where the big cat went.

The panther came up on the porch, sniffed around where she had been sitting, and low and behold, it started lapping up her coffee! After it finished doing that, it stuck its huge head up to her screen door. It was banging its head sort of or rubbing its head against the screen door so that it was making the door rattle.

It sounded to her like maybe the panther was trying to get in the house! She started having a panic attack, thinking about how big the panther was and what would happen if it tried to get in on her. She went to the phone and tried to dial our number. My mamaw answered right away.

Mamaw, Mom, Papaw, and I jumped in a car and went down there as fast as we could! We pulled up as close as we could get to the side of the house. Papaw went around back while we waited.

He brought my Granny out of the house safely out the back door to the car. We didn't see any sign of a panther, but she was so scared, she had to spend the night with us.

She said the panther was bigger than a German shepherd! It was HUGE! She said it was so big it was scary. She noticed how big its eyes were. She said its tail was three or four feet long. We all wished the picture would turn out.

When she told her sister what had happened, her sister didn't exactly believe her. So, she said she wasn't going to tell anybody else. They probably wouldn't believe her either.

We don't know what happened to the picture she tried to take.

We believed her because we saw how scared she was.

Three Big Mountain Lions
Anonymous

My husband worked on a mining sight over in Whitley County, Kentucky off Highway 92, not far past the Bell County Line. He operated one of the big dozer machines.

He went in to work one day and he noticed that every man on the job had a weapon on him. He thought there might have been trouble that he didn't know about like copper thieves or something. Still, it was very odd that every man he saw was wearing a weapon.

Later in the day he asked someone what was going on. The man he asked said that the day before, one of the work crews, the seeders, had seen three big tawny mountain lions on their job site. They appeared right before plain daylight while the fog was still lingering near the ground. Suddenly they broke out of the timberline in plain view.

There was the seeding crew without any protection, with their hoses stretched far away from the truck, out in the wide open. There were three or four men on that crew and everyone one of them saw the three mountain lions running out of the woods and across the opening where they were working.

They got a very good look at what the animals were and there was no mistaking the size, the muscles, or the deep golden color of the cats. All of the men on that crew had no more protection if one of the cats came after them, than to turn their hose on the mountain lion and hope that scared it away.

Apparently, the cats were chasing a deer or some other prey when they came into the open. Three big cats hunting together also seemed unusual.

Every man on the crew, except one, was packing a weapon. The only one who didn't own a pistol had a large hunting knife on him, strapped to his leg. He said he would be going to the pawn shop that payday to get his own pistol.

Wikimedia commons image in public domain by David Shindle, Conservancy of Southwest Florida, July 16, 2006

Beside of Our Car

By Steve Shaky Peck

Our encounter was very brief, but my wife was about two feet away and looked out the car window directly at the animal. We live in Great Cacapon, West Virginia. We were driving one night, not expecting anything unusual.

My wife screamed when she saw the big black cat. I thought the panther was going to run out in front of our car. It was right beside of her door. We were driving a Mini-Cooper and the head of the panther was about half way up the door. It scared the daylights out of her.

When we got home, she ran straight in the house and left me in the driveway. I want to say it was summer time. It was about 12:00 p.m. It happened a couple of years ago and the whole sighting was very fast. My wife is definite that it was a large black cat and not a house cat.

I love nature. I'm ¼ Apache and love nature and spending time in the woods. You stare it straight in the face.

South Carolina Panther

By Michelle Clark

I've seen a panther. It happened in Abbeville County, South Carolina last summer.

A big black cat with a long tail jumped out of the woods and crossed the road in front of me just around 1:00 a.m. I was headed home from visiting my friends.

I called them and told them about what I'd seen and they were like, "Yep! We hear them all the time down here." I hear them around my house in Anderson County, South Carolina, also.

My grandpa saw one when I was little. We live on its route. So, have I seen it? Do I believe it's there? Most definitely!

Three Witnesses

By Tom Newcomer

I saw a panther in either 1968 or 1969. It was in Hampshire County, West Virginia. It happened about 3:00 a.m. on our way to a hunting camp. Three of us saw it.

I was a teenager, but one of the adults we were with was an accomplished hunter who had hunted across North America.

Raleigh County, West Virginia

By Elbert L. Williams

I saw one on Route 3 in Raleigh County, West Virginia in 2008 on my way to work.

Grandpa's Surprise
By Jeffrey Todd Crunkleton

Here's my story. It was in 1969 or 1970 in Rabin County, Georgia. My family's farm is on Bridge Creek.

Every spring and fall for about two weeks this old painter would hang around our farm. My grandmother said we live on its route.

The cat would hunt along the edge of the corn field and scream when it was mad. Those screams scared us! It even scared our good bear dogs from Carolina.

My dad slipped out one night to put an end to the painter's foolishness and began stalking it toward my grandparents' house about 300 yards away. Right when he got close enough to do something to the animal, BOOM! A shotgun went off and just about scared my dad to death!

Unbeknownst to my dad, my grandpa had also slipped out with the same idea. Well, they didn't get the painter, but must have got a little lead in him. He screamed for the next few hours.

This went on from 1968 to 1975. But the painter stayed out of range of my papaw's old .16 gauge. The only facts I have are what I saw with my own two eyes.

Vintage image in public domain

Pennsylvania Panther

By Joseph Meyer

In Pennsylvania the game commission says there are no big cats in the state. But there are too many rural people who have seen them. This is too much evidence to deny.

In Lancaster County, Pennsylvania an Amish family saw three big cats go into a copse of trees on their farm. The Game Commision representatives came in during the night with trucks and trailers. They tranquilized and removed the three big cats. The township supervisor (Steve Mohr) from Bainbridge can testify to this.

A state senator saw one in his field and got pictures.

My friend saw one drag a deer across the highway.

I had a horse attacked and got pictures of the bite and claw marks. Professional big game hunters came and looked at my horse. They confirmed the bite and marks were from a big cat.

The Game Commissioner said my horse scratched herself on barbed wire. There is no barbed wire anywhere on our property.

A big cat was photographed, and the picture was on Facebook from a local businessman. That was near Washington, Pennsylvania.

The big cats are called the most elusive game in North America for a reason.

Everything I mentioned except my friend Mark seeing a big cat drag a deer was in the newspapers.

Deer Watching

By Teresa A. Brown

Initially we were just looking at a field full of deer. There was a gunshot and all of a sudden this long black cat jumped straight up in the air.

That's when we first saw it. We never knew it was there until the gunshot. It had the longest tail I think I'd ever seen.

Robert Huish 1830

The Game Warden's Opinion

By Darryl Messer

The game warden here told me that black panthers aren't here. Some of his field workers told him they had seen them. He still said they are not here.

He also told me there are albino cougar. He said there are albino, but not black panther.

The one I saw had green eyes. All I know is that it was black.

I saw a wildcat on the middle of the road two years ago while riding my Harley down by the lake. It scared me stiff.

I will not be going deer hunting with a bow without take more fire power along.

Instead of calling people names and telling them they didn't see what they know they did see, could it be possible that some of the origins of these big black cats were part of a circus at some point that got away? I think it's very possible because there were many of the small circuses that traveled across the U.S. from town to town.

Whether the black panther are supposed to be here or not, they could be.

No Nighttime Potty for Me!

By Betty Shell Moses

I live in a tiny house back in the woods. There are not any other people close by. I have to go outside into a camper for the bathroom facility at night. Maybe I won't drink a lot of water any more at night! LOL! Scary! I would NOT want to meet one face to face.

Black panthers scream like a woman. I haven't seen or heard one, but as a child my uncle who lived in the bottom land near old McKenzie Highway in Paris, Tennessee could hear one scream out at night.

He made us kids stay in the house after dark. He lived in the bottom land.

A Good Reason for No Photos!

By Rachel Hudson

The reason there are no photos of black panthers is that most of the time a person realizes what they are, they are in front of you and then gone! Next time I see one, I will ask it to stop so I can take a picture!

Shenandoah Valley

By Wendy Kipple

I am not from the Appalachian Mountains. I am from the Shenandoah Valley in Virginia. I saw a black panther in 2007. I understand quite well about being ridiculed.

My father who lived in Hollidaysburg Altoona, Pennsylvania saw a black panther roaming along the edge of the woods on their property in 2006.

A Tawny Mountain Lion

By Rebecca J. Lawson

A tawny mountain lion tried to "catch" me for dinner about twenty-three years ago. The incident took place on Big Mountain in Russell County, Virginia. Luckily, I made it to my vehicle before it jumped. Scary!

1896 Antique Panther Chart

Grandmother's Scars

By Josh Keys

My grandmother lived in a place called Brushy Run, West Virginia in 1900. She told me she was in their garden working when this happened. It was a trace on the side of a mountain on their farm near Seneca Rock, West Virginia in Pendleton County. The old home place is now a park.

A fawn or yellow colored mountain lion attacked her in the garden. Being a large woman of German descent, she fought it and broke loose. She ran for the house screaming for her brothers. One of them shot and killed the cat. She had the scars from the attack for the rest of her life.

She was my mom's grandma and I grew up around her. I'm 38.

My dad and granddaddy were deer hunting near Monterey in Highland County, Virginia in the 1960s. Granddaddy was William F. Keys, and dad is Van Keys.

They spotted a black panther. Being old school, granddaddy wanted to kill it. They tracked it all day, but every time a possible shot was presented, which was at a good distance, the cat ran. They said later that night, they could hear it screaming in the hills like a woman crying and like a baby crying.

My Uncle GG Heavener's son killed a yellow lion on his property in Grant County, West Virginia in the early 2000s. He was a WWII hero of the 82nd AB Division Normandy, Battle of the Bulge. He won the Silver Star and DSC at the Bulge. He didn't know it was illegal to kill the animal and brought the dead cat into town. His buddy told him it was illegal, so he drove back out away from town and dumped it. He has passed away since.

I found tracks of a mother and cubs in Greene County, Virginia in a place called Mutton Holler. I took the pictures to the sheriff and he said they get reports every year of people seeing the big cats in the end of the summer and fall.

Denial is the most pervasive human reaction to anything unfamiliar. I personally took pictures of tracks of a mother and cubs on the border of the Blue Ridge National Forest. This was in Greene County four years ago.

I went to the sheriff's office and showed him the photos. He said they get calls at the end of the summer and early fall every year of mountain lions killing people's livestock. My picture was not a shock to him. Then I showed them to a Game Warden and he said that he had found them, too, and thought he saw one some time ago.

In the same area a friend of mine who is a chief in the RS in Greene had one cross the road in front of him. That was near Rock Fish Gap which is only twenty miles or so from Swift Run Gap near where I found the tracks.

Hawk Creek Road

By Kellie Harris

My sighting was on Hawk Creek Road in London, Kentucky. That's not far from Slate Lick.

I believe sightings are more prominent now due to the loss of the old-time woodsman mountain men. They were men that foraged and hunted and trapped small game to feed their families.

With that generation's lifestyle fading, the number of small game is on the rise. Local forest areas are being revamped and pushing the animals to new areas and giving them less places to hide.

Chipper Mill Black Panther

By Amy Rattler

My encounter took place in Marble, North Carolina.

In 1998 my boyfriend had driven from below the Chipper Mill in Marble to Andres in the snow to pick me up from work. On the way back home, we were driving by the grain bins below the airport and two of the most beautiful black panthers crossed the road right in front of us and jumped up on a wall.

We were driving a Tracker and they came up to about the same height as the hood.

We turned and shined the headlights but couldn't' see anything. We could hear them. We were stupid enough to get out of the car and saw their paw prints in the snow.

Many other people in our area have reported seeing them. My girl's cousin has recently been hearing one. Her sister caught something on video, but when she showed it to the rangers, they said it was just a dog.

Living Behind My House

By Jessica Perry

Sissonville, West Virginia. I have at least one large tan mountain lion living behind my house. I almost hit it with my car once.

I have seen a black panther on Poca River Road. They are HUGE!

East Tennessee

By Wayne Hall

I've seen one in East Tennessee near the Great Smokey Mountain National Park.

A Licken' for Lying

By Jim McIntosh

I saw a black panther in 1966 when I was just a young boy in Wood County, West Virginia. I didn't tell anyone because I figured Pap would give me a licken for lying.

The panther was chasing a small deer around the hill top!

30 Miles North of Cincinnati

By La Sheila R. Chamers

My daughter and I were coming home late one night in the fall some fifteen years ago. About a mile before we got home, a black panther crossed the road in front of us and scared us both.

We live in the country and we are sure of what we saw. We have not seen one since. This was in Ohio, thirty miles north of Cincinnati.

R.G. Badger 1910

I'd Like to Know What It Is!

By Mary Lynn Lethcoe

If they don't exist, then I sure would like to know what it is!! They are certainly NOT overgrown wildcats or house cats.

The one my grandfather saw was BIG and BLACK. He grew up in the country and knew what a bobcat, wildcat, and large regular cats looked like. His sighting was in the wee hours of the morning around 2:00 or 3:00 a.m.

My grandfather was awake and sitting at the kitchen door looking out. He did this frequently when he couldn't sleep. The moon was big, bright, and full. He could see the back yard as if it was day. A large black panther walked across the back yard and into the woods behind his house.

To be explicit in what he said, "Good thing Rosie, we have an inside toilet because if I had been coming from the outhouse, we would be washing clothes this mornin'!

He was pretty darn certain of what he saw! By the way, he was not a "big yarn teller" either!

The Most Graceful Thing

By Elaine and Bobby Philpot

It was many years ago, when I saw a big cat. The lady that was with me has passed away, so I don't have a witness.

We saw it crossing a road in front of us. It was the most graceful thing I'd ever seen. I'm certain it was a cougar, panther, or whatever they want to call it.

It was seen by others in the community after that. I no longer liver there, but someone of the guys that saw it still does.

Momma Panther

By Duane Murphy

I saw one in Pike County, Kentucky with its litter of kittens. Every time one would leave the "nest" she would run out and carry it back. I was up the mountain cliff about forty yards above her on a gas road and watched her for a while.

Panther Cries

By Nick Armrister

I live in the mountains of Virginia. When we were young, we would walk around at night. We'd go camping and stuff in the dark. One night, we were walking down this big hill and the cat was in a big pine tree.

It started crying. We looked up and saw it. We ran like crazy, got to the house, stood on the porch and listened to it cry for hours. It was close to the house.

For years we could hear it cry, but never saw it again, not even once. The scond time I saw one, I was riding by and saw it drinking water from a pond. It sure was scary!

Two Black Ones

By Billy Simpson

I've seen two black panthers. One was in Harlan County going across Pine Mountain when I was a teenager.

I live in Nebraska now. Five years ago I saw one when I in broad daylight.

A Tail for Balance

By Shelby Jean Payne Maxwell.

I saw a black panther once. What surprised me most was how long its tail was and how big its head was.

Once it was in the tree, it crept in complete silence out to the nest and its tail was dropped down and curled like it was using it for balance. It was a most exciting experience.

I am an amateur photographer and her I am on top of a building, looking at the most amazing thing and nobody is going to believe me and my camera is in the truck!

Our local paper had run an ad wanting to know if anybody had seen anything that resembled a mountain lion/cougar, so I asked them if they wanted me to report the sighting. The reporter told me not to.

I was told to let people think there are none in the region. Our area didn't need that kind of attention.

I don't know if the guy really thought that or if he thought other people would think I was crazy.

A Yellow One

By Kirs Ten

I have seen a yellow one in Haysi, Virginia, although it was about fifteen years ago.

Clintwood, Virginia

By Haili Phillips

They are in Clintwood, Virginia – at least the mountain lions.

What I Saw

By Linda Randolph English

I saw one in Tennessee. I had to back up the car to make sure I saw what I thought I saw. Yep. It was a big black panther!

Photo by Judith Victoria Hensley - Bobcat

I Feel Privileged

By Marcia Gabbard

I've seen a black panther in Southeast, Kentucky. It was the most magnificent creature I've ever laid eyes on. It had huge green eyes.

I saw it near a river on my way home from work around 1:00 a.m.

No one believed me, but of course, I don't care. I know what I saw and feel very privileged that I did.

Edward Lloyd 1896

Black Lab

By Vicky Jarrett

My black lab started barking like crazy and I went out to see what the fuss was about. She was fifty yards up the bank above the house. I got up to her and that's when the panther crawled up the side of the tree.

It scared me, the dog, and the panther. There's no mistake it was a black panther. The tree incident was around 2010. That was not my first encounter with one, though.

This incident happened in Clay County, Kentucky. I heard one screaming one night. It sounded like a woman being strangled. It was screaming like crazy.

My father said, "That's a black panther!" This happened in about 1994.

Devil on His Tail

By Donna Buckner Proctor

I have seen a black panther. He was beautiful! He was running like the devil was on his tail.

Welsh Mountain Area

By Jeff Hall

There was an article and picture in the newspaper, in Elizabethtown, Pennsylvania about a panther. Quite a few people said they saw it. I'm guessing it was around 2010.

There were reports all over Welsh Mountain area, New Holland, and Quarryville. One farmer had a goat mauled, and they were finding deer remains in the area.

No one was ever able to confirm what did it.

Soddy Daisy

By Glenda Click

My grandpa told us stories of riding his horse home and one jumped out at him. This happened in Soddy Daisy, Tennessee.

Saw One at Age 50

By Maudie Barnes

I have seen one in South Carolina. I always heard about them but was almost 50 years old when I saw one.

Casey County, Kentucky

By Matt Sam

I have seen one in Casey County, Kentucky. My mother and grandmother have also seen one.

Maidsville, West Virginia

By Judy H. Thompson

I saw one in my back yard thirty something years ago. I lived in Maidsville, West Virginia.

I remember my mother talking about seeing one. She said at night she could hear their cries. She said they sounded like a woman or a child crying.

I heard their cries at night while sitting on my porch.

When you have seen one yourself, it doesn't matter HOW MANY PEOPLE tell you they don't exist!

Western North Carolina

By Dan Eller

I have seen them here on the mountains in Western North Carolina.

Paw-Paw's Tales

By David Slater

My paw-paw from West Virginia used to tell us about panthers up in the mountains.

Clear Signs of Big Cats

By Amber Hobitday

I see clear signs of large cat poop in the mountains, laid down den areas, tufts of hair, soft under fur, things that have been chewed on with sharp looking holes in them, that's not quite bear size holes.

I've noticed hairs, foot tracks in the mud, clawing marks on trees, around bedding down areas. I see clear signs. I believe they are in these West Virginia Eastern Panhandle Mountains. I have witnessed people showing them to me on their deer cams that were deep in the woods.

My Brother Set His Shirt on Fire

By Boyd Coots

A few years ago, my brother and I were camping in the mountians. We heard a cat crying in the woods, sounding like a baby crying. We decided to go, and we walked out at about 12:00 because we knew something was there.

When it showed itself, we clearly saw it was a black panther. We were walking on the road, and it was walking in the woods along beside of the road following us. It hollered like a young baby crying.

It stayed in the woods while we were walking on the road, but it kept making that sound, crying like a baby.

My brother took his shirt off and threw it down in the road and set it on fire. Most animals are afraid of fire, you know. It worked. The panther ran off and we went on home!

Same Signs

By Danny Gordon

I've seen most of the sign that Amber Hobitday spoke of in these messages. Did you ever see a deer carcass twenty-feet up in a tree?

I watched one once stand on his back legs and claw a persimmon tree. The claw marks were seven feet off the ground! He was a big thick cat. I had never seen anything like him!

Rock overhangs with dry dirt underneath them is where you can take a stick and drag the dirt and see their scat! Just thought I'd share this. I can tell Amber has been out an seen these things! I live in North Georgia.

Rydal, Georgia

By Dolly Thorn

I've seen a black panther here in Rydal, Georgia in the Pinelog Mountain WMA.

My aunt has seen them in Western Maryland as well.

Rydal, Georgia, Too

By Kay Mulvihill

I live in Rydal, Georgia. I have never actually seen a black panther, but I have heard several people in the area talk about having seen them. They truly believe they are here.

Camping in Falling Rock

Ramona Hayes Postelwait

In about 1974 or 1975, we were camping up in a holler in Falling Rock, West Virginia. We were near the old swimming hole. Everyone in the area knew this place by that name. My mom, dad, sister, uncle and I were camping.

t was dark and we heard a "woman scream". My dad and uncle jumped up and made us get inside because they were sure it was a panther. People had seen it in the area. My uncle stayed up all night long and burned all our firewood, so it would stay away from the campsite.

On an October Day

By Anne Watkins Tolley

I saw one here in Northeast Tennessee. We have lots of deer, and I had peeled apples to toss over the fence to the woods. It was on an October day in 1998.

I saw a panther. It was sleek and fast. I called a local nature preserve. They didn't believe me. They said it was a bear.

No, it wasn't! That same week I saw a bobcat and we found a dead baby deer. They are in neighboring counties. I know what I saw.

Big Cat Species

By Konnie Downing Conrad

Black panthers are not endangered because the term "black panther" is used for any black cat from a big cat species that is normally spotted. Black panthers are not a species on their own according to wikipedia.

Lookout Mountain

By Andy Johnson

I grew up on Lookout Mountain in Northwest, Georgia. The last black panther I saw was about 1973.

My mother and I were driving through an old coal mining area called Durham. A panther came out of the woods in front of us. We slowed down and it walked beside of the car for about a quarter of a mile. Then it just turned into the woods and it was gone.

We used to hear them all the time. The sound like a woman screaming.

Western North Carolina

By Shelby Christina Houston

I saw one twice in the same spot where I'm at. The sightings occurred over a three-year period in the mountains of Western North Carolina.

Deer Spotting

By Chuck Lecker

We lived on 82 acres in South Carolina back in the early 1990s. We saw a panther one night while spotting deer.

My neighbor down the road said there were two of them on the back property of ours. When the timber had been logged out, they moved onto our property. You could hear them every now and then at night screaming depending on how far away they were on the property.

I had food plots out for deer and we noticed we hadn't been seeing any deer. So, we went spotting one night and that's when we saw one of them. It was lying right by our food plot. Then it stood up.

My wife thought it was our black lab, but when I saw the green eyes and long tail, I knew better. It took off running down our old tram road. We followed it until it went into the woods. We never did see both of them that our neighbors had seen. We only saw just that one.

Black Panther in the Crawl Space

By Vicki Fields

I have a story from my childhood. My daddy knows the details. There was a black panther in our crawl space! I only know I wasn't allowed outside.

This was in 1930 in Asheville, North Carolina.

Granny's Tales

By Donna Marshall

My granny told us kids panther tales all the time. It always scared me to death.

Hit By a Car

By Grace Deel

I saw a yellow one that had been hit by a car near Meadow View, Virginia.

I was way up in the mountains here doing mine security on a mine station. My husband and I saw big cat tracks in a mine tipple. I think they were sleeping there, thinking it was a cave of sorts.

Mamaw's Call

By Becki Morris Thomas

I live in my grandparents' home in Northeast Georgia. There used to be a lot of "painters" in our area. Our family raised beef for food.

The animals (big cats) were going after the cattle. My mamaw could call panthers. She had a scream that sounds exactly like them.

So, at night my grandparents as well as my great uncle (would go outside and Mamaw would "call the painters" so Papaw or Uncle Ed could shoot them.

Sometimes you just have to do whatever is necessary to protect your livestock and feed your family.

FELIS NIGRA

Black Puma 1843 England

Wompas Cats

By Tammy Vandiver Adams

We live in the North Georgia Mountains.

In the 1950s before I was born, my mother went out to the chicken house. When she topped the hill, there lying in the morning sun in front of the chicken house was a huge panther. Mama said it was dark colored, but with the sun shining on its coat, she could see a pattern underneath the dark. Its long tail was twitching.

Mama was afraid to turn around. She was afraid it would jump on her back. Thus, she walked backwards, back to the house. She called my grandpa who lived right out the road, but by the time he got to our house with his gun, it was gone.

My daughter saw one in the laurel thickets also, just a few years ago, in the same area. Grandpa called them Wompas Cats.

Edward Lloyd 1896

Barnes Mountain

By Tiffany Canter

I have seen two of the black mountain lions/panthers. These sightings happened where I'm from in Irvine, Kentucky on Barnes Mountain.

I saw one walking in a field near the edge of the tree line. We knew it wasn't a house cat because even though we were a good distance away, it was still very large.

On another occasion I was at a buddy's house one evening around 8:00 – 0:00 p.m. at night. I was on their porch while she was draining hamburger grease outside. Her son was out there, also.

We grabbed her son and ran back in the house because one came walking across the blacktop. I'm assuming it was coming after a chicken.

I've heard them scream out while walking to my grandparents' house and boy oh boy, you wanna talk about getting the lead out and hauling butt. I never moved so quick!

Also, I remember my father and uncle telling me about a time when they were younger and saw a huge black cat. They said they were driving on the gravel road by the river and stopped to do something. I can't remember what it was or maybe they never said, but anyways, they said that while they were sitting there, a big black cat walked towards the car. It was so big that could have easily put its chin on the bottom of the window had it walked up to the car.

Needless to say, they didn't get out. I know people say they are "extinct" but I've seen them and heard them. Let me tell you, if you hear one scream out, you won't ever forget that sound!

Schubert 1885

Two Sightings

By Wayne Harrah

The first time I saw a panther, I was probably around 19 years old. I was spring gobbler hunting on Usum mountain, as the old timers called it.

I was done hunting and driving around the mountain when something black crossed the road about a hundred yards in front of me. We didn't have any bear in the area at the time, so I thought it was a dog. When it hit the open hillside and slowed down to like a single jumping movement I knew it was a cat.

It was big like a big hound dog would be. Its tail seemed to whip with its movement but was as long as it's body. The whole sighting was probably less than sixty seconds, but I know what I saw.

My second sighting was a few years later. I was traveling between Elton and Meadow Bridge on Route 20 going towards Meadow Bridge. I was going up what is called Elton Mountain.

When I rounded the curve, there was a big black cat sitting on the guard rail. Its tail was hanging in front of it and almost touching the ground. The top of its head I would say three feet tall the way it was sitting.

The next wide spot I came to, I turned around and went back to get a better look, but it was gone. I went about three miles on down the road, stopped and told a friend.

He laughed and asked, "How much have you had to drink?"

I said, "Nothing!"

He wouldn't believe me until about three days later. He was going up the same mountain and about a half a mile from where I had seen it, he saw it walking beside the road. That's all I know of his sighting, but he did apologize to me.

My first one was around 11:00 o'clock in the day. The second one was right at dusk in the fall of the year.

1762 Engraving

Angel Dogs

By Barbara Embree Thomas

I think it was about 1986 when this happened. We had rented a trailer at what the people around here call "Blue Banks." It got that name because of the blue clay in the soil. It is near "Indian Fort Mountain" at Berea, Kentucky.

The public entrance for hiking to the cliffs and all those attractions are on the side closest to Berea. We were situated on the opposite side with a small grassy back yard between the trailer and the high bank on the back side of the mountain. When we moved in, there was a large new dog kennel sitting there at the end of the property with a doghouse in it. We kept thinking previous renters would be back for that nice new kennel, but they never showed up.

One evening before dark, my husband, and our three girls, and I were in the front yard playing when we saw two large beautiful white and black spotted coonhounds coming down the drive. I've got many coon hunters in my family and we knew many that still hunt. So, we just walked to meet them, knowing they were too pretty and well taken care of to not belong to someone.

We put them in the kennel, hoping we'd find out who they belonged to. They had been there with us for weeks, but no one had claimed them.

One sunny day, my husband was at work, and the two older girls were at school. Four-year-old Kelly, our baby, wanted to go out to play. I was cleaning in the kitchen, so I let her go right behind the house. I could see her from the kitchen door I'd left open. She was mostly playing just in middle between the trailer and the bank of the mountain, running and jumping in the grass.

Suddenly the coon hounds went crazy barking. I ran to the back door. My baby had stopped playing and was looking toward the dogs. I looked up on the bank past her amongst the growth of short bushes and tiny trees.

There was a black panther. He was very long with sleek black fur shining. He was watching my baby. Thank God, I thought of how much Kelly loved dogs. (She's 32 now and still does.)

I had to speak clear and calm, so I wouldn't scare her. I just called out like I was playing. "Kelly, go to the pen with the dogs."

I'd never done that before, so she looked at me oddly. I was keeping an eye on the panther. I had to repeat myself to her in a sing-song voice. She went to the pen. She had a little trouble opening the latch, but I sing-songed the way to lift the latch to her, telling her to shut it back so the dogs wouldn't get out. She did it all just right.

The dogs were still jumping and barking at the panther. I looked at him. He was watching the dogs but turned his head and looked straight at me for a few seconds, I guess. Then he whipped up through the brush. The brush was making noises as he went, and he was a black flash going up the mountain.

I always called those coonhounds our "Angel Dogs" after that. We believe they were sent there for that very purpose - to save our beautiful little dark haired, dark eyed girl from that panther.

We never found the owners of the dogs, which was odd for this area. When my dad and little brother (who coon hunted a lot) told us about a man they hunted with, that took the very best care of his dogs, and was an all-around good person, we sent word to see if he wanted them. He came after them.

We moved away shortly after he came for the dogs.

Kelly and I had another panther experience when she was 8 or 9 on the other side of Indian Fort Mountain, but I won't go into that one now. We decided we don't need to be around a mountain together.

We know the panther is still around.

Family History of Panthers

By Rocky Sylvester

We have panthers in our family history. Mother told us of our Great-grandma Smith and the panther that attacked her horse while she was riding. She was able to kill the cat by strangling it with her legs!

During the 1900s another time, a cat had followed an aunt home from "up the holler," and as she entered the property, the cat lit on a fence rail and was killed by her husband. This happened in Carrol County, Virginia a long time ago.

Mother Golda left us in October. I wish I could hear these stories again!!!

Public Domain Image from Wikimedia Commons – Tony Hisgett from Birmingham, UK February 18, 2010

Mountain Story Tellers

By Jerry L. Harmon

I am from a long line of Appalachian mountain people. My great-great grandad was Council Harmon. He is credited by historians to be the first to bring the Jack Tales to America, ie – Jack and the Beanstalk. There are many of those tales and they have been passed through my family for hundreds of years.

Ray Hicks was my cousin. He was declared a National Treasure because of his history. He was a grand story teller.

My dad told me a story of my great-grandpa Link Presness and a mountain lion. I also had my grandma Harmon tell me one.

I have been blessed to share the tales in different countries in Europe, etc. I would like to get a foot in to tell them to the children in the schools of the Appalachians for they need to know about them. Maybe one day I will find a way.

One of the stories was told to me by my grandma, Cindy Harmon. She was a midwife when she was a younger woman. She had traveled through the mountains to be with a woman who was close to child birth. The old shack of a house was not very well structured, and the floor had cracks in it.

The baby was being born and the blood smell reached a panther who came under the house. Grandmother said the panther was tearing at the boards and had made some headway near the fireplace. The older son of the lady giving birth had to chunk hot cinders at the panther's face through the cracks to keep it from coming in the house.

The other story I was told by my dad. My Great-grandpa, Link Presnell, was a legend in the mountains of Tennessee. My father said Grandpa was out hunting one night with his dogs, but he was just listening to the dogs run and did not have a gun. He got tired and just laid down for the night. He did this often and carried a quilt rolled up for a bed.

He was starting to sleep when he heard a panther scream pretty close by. He got up and built up a fire. He had to keep the fire going all night long to keep the "painter" away from him. Dad said Grandpa Link told about how the panther would get so close he could see its eyes shining in the trees but knew the panther would not get any closer as long as he kept the fire going.

Eventually, it left.

Camera in the Truck

By Shelby Jean Payne Maxwell

My nephew saw a black panther near his property. He was with his brother-in-law when they saw it. They are really nice young men, and both are hunters who were raised in the mountains. They definitely know the difference between a black panther and a dog or any other animal.

I saw one. What surprised me most was how long its tail was and how big its head was. Once it was in the tree, it crept in complete silence out to the nest and its tail was dropped down and curled like it was using it for balance. That was a most exciting experience!

I am an amateur photographer and there I was on top of a building looking at the most amazing thing and nobody was going to believe me! My camera was in my truck!

Our local paper ran an ad wanting to know if anybody had seen anything that resembled a mountain lion or cougar. So, I asked the gentleman if he wanted me to report it, and he told me not to.

"Let them think there are none in the area. Our area doesn't need that kind of attention."

I don't know if he truly thought that or if he thought they would think I was crazy!

A herd of elk has been released in my county. I haven't been to see them yet but am planning on taking my grandson to see them. I shoot phots mostly of horses and horse shows, but would surely like to have had just one shot of that cat.

A few years before that, I had an elderly man who was an avid hunter tell me he killed one (a yellow one). He had an S10 pickup and he said it was as long as the tail gate, and its "eye teeth" were over an inch long and its claw were 2 inches. He just kind of laughed it off.

I never really believed him then, but now I do!

Marcus De Bye or (Marcus De Bie): A seventeenth century Dutch etcher and painter of animals 1660.

Sounded Like A Woman Wailing for Her Baby

By Flora McKenzie

I am a retired nurse and was raised at the foot of a mountain in the Shenandoah Valley of Virginia. All my life I was told that a panther sounded like a woman crying.

In 1989 I moved to a cabin near Trout Pond in Lost River, West Virginia. It was just me, my wolf dog, Hekate, and my rifle.

One night I heard the most haunting "scream," if that is what you would call it. My dog started howling like crazy. The screaming continued. It sounded so pitiful! It sounded like a woman wailing when her child had died.

I was too scared to go investigate, so I called my nearest neighbor who had lived there his whole life. I asked him what in the world was outside. He told me it was a panther in heat.

A couple of days later it was on the news that the Department of Fish and Wildlife officials had caught it and I forget where they took it. This was in the Spring of 1989 and it was in the Moorefield, West Virginia paper and

on the Channel 3 news in Harrisonburg,
Virginia.

I hope to never hear anything that
mournful again! I remember being so scared
because it was so close. I slept with my
shotgun beside of the bed that night because I
had no idea if it would try to break in my cabin.

Robert Huish 1830

Westerville, Ohio

By Andrew Noble

In 1978 or 1979, in the area where I grew up, a few miles north of Westerville, Ohio, there were reported sightings of what was supposedly a large animal. It was believed to possibly be a panther based on descriptions. From what I remember, there was not a close-up sighting for a positive identification of said animal.

Then one night I was driving home, about to turn on the road I lived on, about a mile from home. Near the end of the illumination of my headlights, silhouetted in the headlights of an oncoming car, an animal taller than what the headlights of this car were, slinked across the road. This animal had a long tail and moved the same way a cat strolls when walking.

I was on my way home from a school function, probably working on building a set for a play or a football game. So, it probably would have been mid autumn (October?) about 8:00 to 10:00 PM. I remember it wasn't cold and the trees still had leaves.

I told my Mom about it when I got home. She suggested I report this to the Delaware County Sheriff. When I called, they were kind of "yeah, yeah" until I told them where I saw it.

Then they were very interested and listened to my report.

The next morning, while I was at school, my Mom and the local game warden went to where I saw it and looked around. They found fresh prints that appeared to be of a large cat. My Mom made a plaster cast of one of the prints. She took it to an authority on tracks (to the zoo maybe?), to have it identified. It was positively identified as a panther.

I have no idea what ever happened to the casting. Or where the cat ended up.

1830 John Huish

Indian Fort in Berea, Kentucky

By Susan Mullins

I personally haven't had any encounters with black panther, but there were several sightings at the Miller Welch Wildlife Management area in Berea, Kentucky. A friend of mine said she was walking her dog for exercise.

She said she had seen a large black cat watching them from the brush. She said it was too big to be a house cat. She described it as the size of a Great Dane.

There were too many cars going by at the time for the big cat to show itself openly. She figured all the traffic kept it in the bush. She still hikes but not alone anymore.

There are a lot of horse activities through the year. There are dog trails, horseback riding, dove hunts etc. in the area. This sighting happened a few years ago. She still walks the trails but hasn't seen the panther since the one incident. However, several others have seen it.

It would be possible to have large cats in the area. There are miles of woodlands behind the town of Berea. The hills behind Indian Fort area have many caves. The area goes all the way on the back roads where there are only a few houses here and there through Jackson County and Clay County, Kentucky.

There are towns in between but plenty of room for big cats. I know for sure of bobcats being in the area. Our barn cat had a litter with several kittens with bob tails.

Bears were introduced to areas in Tennessee. Many bears have been spotted in Kentucky. Wild animals such as bear and big cats are very intelligent. With shortages of food, we see them looking for food in more developed areas, but when all is well in the wild you can bet they see us more than we see them.

By John Huish 1830

Bearmeat Mountain

By Renee Smithey

I now live in Murphy, North Carolina. We recently moved from Hiawassee, Georgia. We lived for four years there on Bearmeat Mountain. I saw a black panther there twice during the last year we were there.

The first time I saw it (not sure if it was the same one, mind you). It was at night and I was going out the driveway. I was alone. I only saw the back half as it was going into the woods, but I knew it was too tall and the tail was too long to be a housecat.

The second time I saw one was a few days later in broad daylight. This was during summer because I was canning. I saw it moseying across the pasture behind our house. I quickly got my son up to see it. By the time we got back to the kitchen window it was sitting in tall grass near a pig barn. We watched for a long while but it didn't move.

My son never believed me. He never saw it clearly. He never saw how big it was.

Neighbors who had lived in the neighborhood all their lives thought it ay have come down from the peaks to get away from the wildfire. I never heard it make a sound. A lot of longtime residents here have seen and heard them.

Southeast Ohio

By Heather Heart

My mom (M. Sharon Wisecup), and I saw one about 35 years ago. He was just walking up the side of the road. It was dark out, but we both knew what we saw.

We both looked at each other and said, "Did you see what I saw?"

We knew no one would believe us. Through the years I've heard many stories of people seeing them around here. We are in Southeast Ohio.

Cat Creek

By Angela Oldfield

We have a road called Cat Creek here, just outside of Stanton, Kentucky. Residents have claimed for decades that there are black panthers in the hills up there.

November

By Debbie Akers

I saw one in November. My grandson was bringing me home. As we were coming up the driveway, it came running down in front of us. It was a very big black cat for sure!

Two at My Home

By Kim Robinson Neal

I've seen two panthers at my home. I have a pond on my property and when I pulled into my driveway, I caught a glimpse from the headlights. Both sightings were at night.

It headed over a very steep embankment that no animal in their right mind would travel. They were very fast and elusive.

These happened in eastern Kentucky.

Photos by Judith Victoria Hensley – Pine Mountain, Kentucky

Foot is an adult size 7

Craigsville, Virginia

By Joseph Edgar Rowland

The first time we saw the big cat was on August 4, 2003, about a mile or so from my home in Craigsville, Virginia. I got photos that are kind of grainy, but I believe you can tell clearly what the animal is. A number of other people saw the cat and started calling The Department of Game and Inland Fisheries. (The Game Commission Office is in Richmond, Virginia.)

The next time I saw the cat was on July 19, 2004 in the field in front of my home. It was time for deer fawns to be born. When I first saw it in the grass, I thought it was a deer giving birth. So, I wen tot my house and got my camera. When I got back and started slowly walking closer to get a better photo, much to my surprise, the cat jumped up and started running away from me.

I help up the camera and snapped a few photos as I was running away.

I notified the Game Commission. When they came out to get the information, they set up cameras to try and get a photo of the cat by using meat. It was a joke, the things they did.

Then they tried to play it off as a large bobcat with a baby groundhog in its mouth. Next, they tried to claim that it must have been an illegal pet and someone got tired of feeding it and just released it.

About a month later, a man named John A. Lutz from the Eastern Puma Research Network based in Maysville, West Virginia came to my home and spent the day looking at the photos and examining the area where the cat had been seen. He made the statement that without a shadow of doubt it was indeed a puma/mountain lion.

Photos by Joe Rowland – Craigsville, Virginia – July 19, 2014

Confederate Gold – Folklore
Oral Story Telling Traditional Story

Public domain photo of a bronze panther

*For decades a rumor circulated about
Confederate gold that was hidden in a cave in
the mountains along the Kentucky and Virginia
border. It was reported that among the treasure
was a solid gold statue of Gen. Robert E. Lee
riding on the back of a black panther. As far as
anyone knows, the stash has never been
recovered. (Local folklore)*

A Lot of Time in the Woods
An Interview with Thomas Marcum

I spend a lot of time in the mountains and do a lot of research on location in the mountains. I dig ginseng in season, and sometimes I just enjoy exploring.

I'll tell you first about a panther sighting that took place while I was ginsenging last summer in 2017. I usually ride my ATV. As I was riding back one of these hollow roads and when I turned a curve, there standing in the middle the road was a black panther.

I am very familiar with the wildlife in this area. It wasn't quite full grown, but it did have the big long tail. As quick as it saw me, it shot off to the left and up a cut where it looked like a little stream had been running down the mountain. I shot up there on my ATV and got another glimpse of it as it was going up that little creek.

There are also yellow ones here, from many reports, although I have not seen them. I had a report of one from my cousin and uncle as they were cutting timber on their property.

This incident happened about two years ago or maybe three when they were clearing timber on their property. It was during the day time and a large yellow cougar passed by the area where they were working and also had three or four cubs with it. That lets me know there are also males here if they are producing offspring. Breeding couples of the big cats will surely produce more.

The first sighting is about my extent of personal encounters with panther or cougar, although bobcat sightings are fairly common. Both incidents took place in Bell Couty close to the Harlan County line.

I have heard many other tales from people about seeing big cats in this area. My second cousin, who is a little older than I am was talking about things he'd seen while he was working at the coal mine. Some of the men said they had seen black panther in the area.

He said they would often hear what they believed to be a panther screaming at night. They always described it as sounding like a woman screaming. That was at a coal mine in Pathfork which is actually in Harlan County.

My papaw used to ride horses a lot. He is dead and gone now, but I remember his stories. He said that panthers would actually go through the trees and follow them on horseback. They followed on the ground sometimes, but they also literally followed people in the trees, moving from one tree to the next without coming down to the ground.

In the old days the canopy of trees was so thick and the trees were so huge, their branches would intermingle. The big cats could go from the branches of one big tree to the branches of the next without any trouble.

Back in those days, say in the 1950s, they did logging also, but they did not have the equipment we have now. The same thing is true of coal mining. We can tear out a mountain now in no time. Back then it took a lot more time and the trees were much thicker.

He also talked about hearing their eerie scream and how it would scare a person half to death. He and his family and friends would camp out in the mountains a lot. They'd take those long rides on horseback to get to their camping place and saw a lot more from horseback or on foot than what people would see these days passing by on an ATV road or in a bigger vehicle.

They stayed outside a lot. They saw a lot and knew a lot.

There are plenty of tales from people in this area who have personally seen and clear sightings of big cats. There was actually a picture of one on a game camera from over around Pineville. It was a big black cougar. Some people try to say it is just an old housecat. There is a big tree stump visible in the photo for scale, but it's hard to say from looking at the photo how big the tree stump is, therefore impossible to say exactly how big the cat is.

I run game cameras all year round looking for big game and wildlife, or unusual things like that. I have not caught a cougar yet on camera, but I have gotten pictures of black foxes. That is really a rare animal. I have two of those on game camera together.

This animal is seen a lot in Florida, but not much around here, namely a black bobcat. They are common in Florida, but they are not seen here very often. I saw one about seven or eight years ago. We were logging and it was in the daytime, so we got a very good look at it. It looked just like a regular bobcat, but it was black. It would be possible for someone to mistake one from a great distance as a panther, but we know the panther is much bigger and has the long tail, unlike the bobcat.

Because I do other research, do ginseng hunting, and things of that nature, I spend a lot of time in the woods. A lot. I enjoy any form of cryptid research.

Thomas Marcum is the founder of The Crypto Crew, a cryptozoology research organization. Thomas has over 20 years of experience conducting research in the field. He has more than a few stories he can tell you. In 2014, he was the paranormal awards winner for both picture of the year, and investigator of the year. Follow his latest discoveries at **http://www.thecryptocrew.com/**.

Two in One Day
By Elizabeth Skinner

Not many are going to believe this (I wouldn't either if I didn't have these photos and seen them with my own eyes) because the Internet will tell you we don't have black panthers in North Carolina.

Today we saw not one, but two, black panthers/cougars. One was off of Pea Ridge Road by my house and the other was on Highway 32 outside of Roper. We thought they were bear, that's how large they were, until I looked at the tail.

A dead panther 1870s, in the area of Jupiter Lighthous.
Photo from the Historical Society of Palm Beach County

Vintage image of mountain lion hunt – Public domain

Vermont Historical Society

*Alexander Crowell and the Panther he killed in 1881. Public domain
photo. The animal was called panther and catamount in Vermont
where it was killed.*

Big Cats and Public Safety Protection Act

On September 17, 2012 John Kerry (Democrat from Massachusetts) introduced S.3547, known as the Big Cats and Public Safety Protection Act. This act was aimed at prohibiting private possession and breeding of captive big cats in the United States. The House version of the bill was introduced by U.S. Representatives Buck McKeon (Republican from California) and Loretta Sanchez (Democrat from California in 2013. (Public record)

The motivation behind this action resulted from the animal massacre in Zanesville, Ohio in 2011 (documented in multiple news sources across the nation) when the owner of the exotic animals freed his animals from their cages into the public arena, then committed suicide. This release of dangerous wildlife into the public resulted in the necessary slaughter by police officials of nearly 50 animals. Of those 59, 38 were big cats. The euthanasia of these animals was necessary for public safety.

Many states already ban private ownership of exotic animals, but some have only partial bans, and others have absolutely no restrictions. The inconsistency may not seem that crucial until one realizes that there are estimated to be from between 10,000 and 20,000 big cats currently held in private ownership in the U.S. This number does not include all of the big cats in captivity that no one knows about. (Information available from Bigcatrescue.org)

The 2015 version of the Big Cat Public Safety Act HR3546/S2541 Was introduced to the House on September 17, 2015 by representative Walter Jones (Republican fro North Carolina). Senator Richard Blumenthal (democrat from Connecticut introduced the bill in the Senate on February 11, 2016.

A copy of the bill is included below directly from **www.congress.gov** (Public Record)

115TH CONGRESS 1ST SESSION H. R. 1818

To amend the Lacey Act Amendments of 1981 to clarify provisions enacted by the Captive Wildlife Safety Act, to further the conservation of certain wildlife species, and for other purposes.

IN THE HOUSE OF REPRESENTATIVES MARCH 30, 2017 Mr. DENHAM (for himself, Mr. JONES, Mr. FARENTHOLD, Mr. LOBIONDO, Mr. GAETZ, Ms. TSONGAS, Mr. ROSS, and Mr. JOHNSON of Ohio) introduced the following bill; which was referred to the Committee on Natural Resources

A BILL To amend the Lacey Act Amendments of 1981 to clarify provisions enacted by the Captive Wildlife Safety Act, to further the conservation of certain wildlife species, and for other purposes.

Be it enacted by the Senate and House of Representa-1 tives of the United States of America in Congress assembled, 2 SECTION 1. SHORT TITLE. 3 This Act may be cited as the "Big Cat Public Safety 4 Act". 5

VerDate Sep 11 2014 04:28 Apr 04, 2017 Jkt 069200 PO 00000 Frm 00001 Fmt 6652 Sfmt 6201 E:\BILLS\H1818.IH H1818 lotter on DSK5VPTVN1PROD with BILLS

2

•HR 1818 IH

SEC. 2. DEFINITIONS. 1 (a) IN GENERAL.—Section 2 of the Lacey Act 2 Amendments of 1981 (16 U.S.C. 3371) is amended— 3 (1) by redesignating subsections (a) through (k) 4 as subsections (b) through (l), respectively; and 5 (2) by inserting before subsection (b) (as so re-6 designated) the following: 7 "(a) BREED.—The term 'breed' means to facilitate 8 propagation or reproduction (whether intentionally or neg-9 ligently), or to fail to prevent propagation or reproduc-10 tion.". 11 (b) CONFORMING AMENDMENTS.— 12 (1) CONSOLIDATED FARM AND RURAL DEVEL-13 OPMENT ACT.—Section 349(a)(3) of the Consoli-14 dated Farm and Rural Development Act (7 U.S.C. 15 1997(a)(3)) is amended by striking "section 2(a)" 16 and inserting "section 2(b)". 17 (2) LACEY ACT AMENDMENTS OF 1981.— 18 (A) Section 3(e)(2)(C) of the Lacey Act 19 Amendments of 1981 (16 U.S.C. 20 3372(e)(2)(C)) is amended— 21 (i) in clause (ii), by striking "section 22 2(g)" and inserting "section 2(h)"; and 23 (ii) in clause (iii), by striking "section 24 2(g)" and inserting "section 2(h)". 25

VerDate Sep 11 2014 04:28 Apr 04, 2017 Jkt 069200 PO 00000 Frm 00002 Fmt 6652 Sfmt 6201 E:\BILLS\H1818.IH H1818 lotter on DSK5VPTVN1PROD with BILLS

3

•HR 1818 IH

(B) Section 7(c) of the Lacey Act Amend-1 ments of 1981 (16 U.S.C. 3376(c)) is amended 2 by striking "section 2(f)(2)(A)" and inserting 3 "section 2(g)(2)(A)". 4 SEC. 3. PROHIBITIONS. 5 Section 3 of the Lacey Act

Amendments of 1981 (16 6 U.S.C. 3372) is amended— 7 (1) in subsection (a)— 8 (A) in paragraph (2)— 9 (i) in subparagraph (A), by striking 10 the semicolon at the end and inserting "; 11 or"; 12 (ii) in subparagraph (B)(iii), by strik-13 ing "; or" and inserting a semicolon; and 14 (iii) by striking subparagraph (C); 15 and 16 (B) in paragraph (4), by striking "(1) 17 through (3)" and inserting "(1) through (3) or 18 subsection (e)"; and 19 (2) by amending subsection (e) to read as fol-20 lows: 21 "(e) CAPTIVE WILDLIFE OFFENSE.— 22 "(1) IN GENERAL.—It is unlawful for any per-23 son to import, export, transport, sell, receive, ac-24 quire, or purchase in interstate or foreign commerce, 25

VerDate Sep 11 2014 04:28 Apr 04, 2017 Jkt 069200 PO 00000 Frm 00003 Fmt 6652 Sfmt 6201 E:\BILLS\H1818.IH H1818 lotter on DSK5VPTVN1PROD with BILLS

4

•HR 1818 IH

or in a manner substantially affecting interstate or 1 foreign commerce, or to breed or possess, any pro-2 hibited wildlife species. 3 "(2) LIMITATION ON APPLICATION.—Paragraph 4 (1) does not apply to— 5 "(A) an entity exhibiting animals to the 6 public under a Class C license from the Depart-7 ment of Agriculture and that holds such license 8 in good standing, if the entity— 9 "(i) has not been, and does not em-10 ploy any person engaged in animal care 11 who has been, convicted of or fined for an 12 offense involving the abuse or neglect of 13 any animal pursuant to any

State, local, or 14 Federal law; 15 "(ii) has not had, and does not em-16 ploy any person who has had, a license or 17 permit regarding the care, possession, exhi-18 bition, breeding, or sale of animals revoked 19 or suspended by any State, local, or Fed-20 eral agency, including the Department of 21 Agriculture, within the preceding 3-year 22 period; 23 "(iii) has not been cited by the De-24 partment of Agriculture under the Animal 25

VerDate Sep 11 2014 04:28 Apr 04, 2017 Jkt 069200 PO 00000 Frm 00004 Fmt 6652 Sfmt 6201 E:\BILLS\H1818.IH H1818 lotter on DSK5VPTVN1PROD with BILLS

5

•HR 1818 IH

Welfare Act (7 U.S.C. 2131 et seq.) within 1 the preceding 12-month period for any re-2 peat violation for— 3 "(I) inadequate veterinary care; 4 "(II) handling that causes stress 5 or trauma or a threat to public safety; 6 "(III) insufficient provisions of 7 food or water; or 8 "(IV) failure to allow facility in-9 spection; 10 "(iv) does not allow any individual 11 other than a trained professional employee 12 or contractor of the licensee (or an accom-13 panying employee receiving professional 14 training) or a licensed veterinarian (or an 15 accompanying veterinary student) to come 16 into direct physical contact with a prohib-17 ited wildlife species; 18 "(v) ensures that during public exhi-19 bition of a lion (Panthera leo), tiger 20 (Panthera tigris), leopard (Panthera 21 pardus), snow leopard (Uncia uncia), jag-22 uar (Panthera onca), cougar (Puma 23 concolor), or any hybrid thereof, the ani-24 mal is at least 15 feet from members of 25

VerDate Sep 11 2014 04:28 Apr 04, 2017 Jkt 069200 PO 00000 Frm 00005 Fmt 6652 Sfmt 6201 E:\BILLS\H1818.IH H1818 lotter on DSK5VPTVN1PROD with BILLS

6

•HR 1818 IH

the public unless there is a permanent bar-1 rier that prevents public contact or risk of 2 contact; 3 "(vi) does not breed any prohibited 4 wildlife species unless the breeding is con-5 ducted pursuant to a species-specific, pub-6 licly available, peer-reviewed population 7 management plan developed according to 8 established conservation science principles; 9 "(vii) maintains liability insurance in 10 an amount of not less than $250,000 for 11 each occurrence of property damage, bodily 12 injury, or death caused by any prohibited 13 wildlife species possessed by the person; 14 and 15 "(viii) has a written plan that is made 16 available to local law enforcement, State 17 agencies and Federal agencies on request, 18 for the quick and safe recapture or de-19 struction of prohibited wildlife species in 20 the event a prohibited wildlife species es-21 capes, including, but not limited to, written 22 protocols for training staff on methods of 23 safe recapture of the escaped prohibited 24 wildlife species; 25

VerDate Sep 11 2014 04:28 Apr 04, 2017 Jkt 069200 PO 00000 Frm 00006 Fmt 6652 Sfmt 6201

E:\BILLS\H1818.IH H1818 lotter on
DSK5VPTVN1PROD with BILLS

7

•HR 1818 IH

"(B) a State college, university, or agency, 1 or State-
licensed veterinarian; 2 "(C) a wildlife sanctuary that
cares for 3 prohibited wildlife species, and— 4 "(i) is a
corporation that is exempt 5 from taxation under
section 501(a) of the 6 Internal Revenue Code of 1986
and de-7 scribed in sections 501(c)(3) and 8
170(b)(1)(A)(vi) of such Code; 9 "(ii) does not
commercially trade in 10 prohibited wildlife species,
including off-11 spring, parts, and byproducts of such
ani-12 mals; 13 "(iii) does not breed the prohibited 14
wildlife species; 15 "(iv) does not allow direct contact be-
16 tween the public and prohibited wildlife 17 species;
and 18 "(v) does not allow the transportation 19 and
display of prohibited wildlife species 20 off-site; 21 "(D)
has custody of the prohibited wildlife 22 species solely
for the purpose of expeditiously 23 transporting the
prohibited wildlife species to a 24

VerDate Sep 11 2014 04:28 Apr 04, 2017 Jkt 069200
PO 00000 Frm 00007 Fmt 6652 Sfmt 6201
E:\BILLS\H1818.IH H1818 lotter on
DSK5VPTVN1PROD with BILLS

8

•HR 1818 IH

person described in this paragraph with respect 1 to the
species; or 2 "(E) an entity or individual that is in pos-3
session of a prohibited wildlife species that was 4 born

before the date of the enactment of the 5 Big Cat Public Safety Act, and— 6 "(i) not later than 180 days after the 7 date of the enactment of the Big Cat Pub-8 lic Safety Act, the entity or individual reg-9 isters each individual animal of each pro-10 hibited wildlife species with the United 11 States Fish and Wildlife Service; 12 "(ii) does not breed, acquire, or sell 13 any prohibited wildlife species after the 14 date of the enactment of such Act; and 15 "(iii) does not allow direct contact bc-16 tween the public and prohibited wildlife 17 species.". 18 SEC. 4. PENALTIES. 19 (a) CIVIL PENALTIES.—Section 4(a)(1) of the Lacey 20 Act Amendments of 1981 (16 U.S.C. 3373(a)(1)) is 21 amended— 22 (1) by inserting "(e)," after "(d),"; and 23 (2) by inserting ", (e)," after "subsection (d)". 24

VerDate Sep 11 2014 04:28 Apr 04, 2017 Jkt 069200 PO 00000 Frm 00008 Fmt 6652 Sfmt 6201 E:\BILLS\H1818.IH H1818 lotter on DSK5VPTVN1PROD with BILLS

9

•HR 1818 IH

(b) CRIMINAL PENALTIES.—Section 4(d) of the 1 Lacey Act Amendments of 1981 (16 U.S.C. 3373(d)) is 2 amended— 3 (1) in paragraph (1)(A), by inserting "(e)," 4 after "(d),"; 5 (2) in paragraph (1)(B), by inserting "(e)," 6 after "(d),"; 7 (3) in paragraph (2), by inserting "(e)," after 8 "(d),"; and 9 (4) by adding at the end the following: 10 "(4) Any person who knowingly violates sub-11 section (e) of section 3 shall be fined not more than 12 $20,000, or imprisoned for not more than five years, 13 or both.

Each violation shall be a separate offense 14 and the offense shall be deemed to have been com-15 mitted not only in the district where the violation 16 first occurred, but also in any district in which the 17 defendant may have taken or been in possession of 18 the prohibited wildlife species.". 19 SEC. 5. FORFEITURE OF PROHIBITED WILDLIFE SPECIES. 20 Section 5(a)(1) of the Lacey Act Amendments of 21 1981 (16 U.S.C. 3374(a)(1)) is amended by inserting 22 "bred, possessed," before "imported, exported,". 23

VerDate Sep 11 2014 04:28 Apr 04, 2017 Jkt 069200 PO 00000 Frm 00009 Fmt 6652 Sfmt 6201 E:\BILLS\H1818.IH H1818 lotter on DSK5VPTVN1PROD with BILLS

10

•HR 1818 IH

SEC. 6. ADMINISTRATION. 1 Section 7(a) of the Lacey Act Amendments of 1981 2 (16 U.S.C. 3376(a)) is amended by adding at the end the 3 following: 4 "(3) The Secretary shall, in consultation with 5 other relevant Federal and State agencies, promul-6 gate any regulations necessary to implement section 7 3(e).". 8

From the Author

I am a story gatherer. I have been collecting panther stories for years with the intent of publishing them in a book. In February 2018 I wondered how many people on the *Appalachian Americans* Facebook page might acknowledge having seen a black panther or a cougar and want to share their experiences in my book. The responses from that post came pouring in within just a couple of days, so many I had to take the post down because I couldn't respond to all. These stories plus the ones I have gathered from personal interviews over the years make up this book and include my own encounters.

This was the Facebook post:

"I'm working on a book called "Panther Tales." I've been collecting stories for years. Many people will tell me their tale, but don't want it in print because they've been ridiculed. I have personally seen BLACK PANTHER mountain lions, (also called painters in these parts) and I know they still exist. I have not seen a yellow one close enough to be 100% sure it was a cougar or yellow/tawny mountain lion. I am positive about the black ones I've seen. If anyone on here is interested in telling your story for this book, I'd love to hear from you. Private message me and I'll send my e-mail. I'm speaking at the Harlan Crypto Con in April and I'd love to have more stories from Harlan, Kentucky and other parts of Appalachia."

The post had 622 Reactions,123 Shares, and 330 Comments. I've tried to include all that I could on these pages and am very thankful for the stories that came in from Appalachia and beyond. Because of the number of stories, one book is not enough to hold all. Volume II is anticipated.

Disclaimer

This book is not, or never will be intended to be a source of scientific evidence as deemed necessary by the scientific community to establish a new species or the acknowledgement of an old one. The author is a story gatherer. Accounts shared in this book are incidents and encounters told by the individual story tellers as truth and compiled for this body of work.

The author believes the stories contained in these pages are true encounters, based on her own experiences and the integrity of the people who shared their stories on these pages. The request was put forth for true stories only. The verity of each story included is the responsibility of the individual story teller.

Scientists demand DNA samples, video, photos, or a literal body of a panther before they will concede the existence of such a creature in this region. The hundreds or perhaps thousands of eyewitnesses' accounts reported across the Appalachian region and beyond are said to be mistaken identity by those in the scientific community who have not personally seen one.

As a reader, or as one who has actually seen a black panther or other big cats in the wild, the opportunity is put before you to make up your own mind.

Image from CCO - Creative Commons Public Domain

If you have a story about your own eyewitness encounter of a big cat, or a story you know from a reliable source (such as family stories handed down), that you would like to contribute to an upcoming book, please follow the guideline below. You must fill out and sign the form on the following page and submit it with your digital signature or via snail mail before your story will be considered. Original artwork/photographs will also be considered.

Please answer these questions.

1. Tell a little about yourself (short), such as job, time spent in the woods, etc.
2. When did the encounter take place?
   - Time of Day
   - Season of the year or month, date if you have it
3. Where did the event take place? (as specifically as possible)
4. Were you with anyone else at the time of the encounter and did they also see the creature?
5. What were you doing at the time of the sighting/encounter?
6. Describe what you saw, especially how the creature looked or behaved.
7. Describe your reaction to the event and the reaction of other people if appropriate.

THERE IS NO PAYMENT FOR STORIES ACCEPTED. IT IS STRICTLY ON A VOLUNTARY BASIS FROM PEOPLE WHO WOULD LIKE TO SEE THEIR STORY IN PRINT and share them with other interested readers/researchers, but the story still belongs to you.

Completed book projects will be available on Amazon.com and Kindle

PANTHER TALES AND WOODLAND ENCOUNTERS II

I, _____, am submitting my
story and/or artwork for consideration in a future
book project about panthers and other big cat sightings.
I will be notified when the project is completed if my
story and/or artwork is included.

I understand that there will be **no purchase of my
story individually or my original artwork**, and **NO
CASH PAYMENT for my story/artwork** and that I am
submitting it strictly on a voluntary basis because I
want to share the story/artwork in print with full credit
given to me for my story and/or artwork. The story will
remain my own intellectual property.

*(There may be editing purposes for grammar,
punctuation, and space within the book set-up, but the
actual story will not be altered in any other way. I trust
the integrity of the story teller to be truthful and share
ONLY non-fiction accounts. – Judith Victoria Hensley)*

_____
Signature   Date

_____
Printed name as you wish it to appear in the book

_____
Address

_____

Submit digitally to: **judith99@bellsouth.net**
Submit by post office mail to: **Judith V. Hensley   P.O.
Box 982   Loyall, KY   40854**

Made in the USA
Monee, IL
10 March 2023